ANDREW MURRAY

Apostle of
abiding love

ANDREW MURRAY
Apostle of
abiding love

Leona Choy

CHRISTIAN LITERATURE CRUSADE
Fort Washington, Pennsylvania 19034

CHRISTIAN LITERATURE CRUSADE
Fort Washington, Pennsylvania 19034

CANADA
1757 Avenue Road, Toronto, Ontario M5M 3YB

GREAT BRITAIN
The Dean, Alresford, Hampshire

AUSTRALIA
P.O. Box 91, Pennant Hills, N.S.W. 2120

ISBN 0-87508-367-6 (Paper)
ISBN 0-87508-368-4 (Cloth)

Printed in the United States of America

ACKNOWLEDGMENT

TO GOD — for the opportunity and the enabling to write this book. All glory to Him.

TO MY PUBLISHER — for the mingled pain and joy of a deadline and the freedom to create as I felt led.

TO PREVIOUS BIOGRAPHERS OF ANDREW MURRAY — that I could reap their diligent labors in part and preserve their fruits.

TO MY HUSBAND — for encouragement, willingness to eat leftovers, and pick strawberries by himself this year.

O GOD OF BETHEL
(The Murray family hymn)

O God of Bethel, by whose hand
Thy people still are fed,
Who through this weary pilgrimage
Hast all our fathers led,

Our vows, our prayers, we now present
Before thy Throne of grace;
God of our fathers, be the God
Of their succeeding race.

Through each perplexing path of life
Our wandering footsteps guide;
Give us each day our daily bread,
And raiment fit provide.

O spread thy covering wings around
Till all our wanderings cease,
And at our Father's loved abode
Our souls arrive in peace.

Such blessings from thy gracious hand
Our humble prayers implore;
And thou shalt be our chosen God,
And portion evermore.

Stanzas 1-4 by Philip Doddridge, 1737
Stanza 5 by John Logan, 1781

CONTENTS

PREFACE
PORTRAIT BY PEN
INTRODUCTION
 1 SAILING TOWARD NEW HORIZONS 19
 2 DEEP ROOTS FOR STRONG TREES 23
 3 STURDY BRANCHES SPREAD........................31
 4 CHOCOLATE CLUB AND LONG GOUDA PIPES 39
 5 UNDER THE WING OF MOTHER CHURCH...........47
 6 WILD DOGS AND EVEN WILDER MEN..............51
 7 VACATIONS FOR SPIRITUAL TREK 55
 8 COVERED WAGON HONEYMOON 61
 9 "A NEW IDEA OF A WIFE" 69
10 REVIVAL AT LAST 77
11 FRUIT THAT REMAINS.............................89
12 URBAN PARISH AND COURT BATTLES...............95
13 WELLINGTON — PASTORATE IN A PASTURE 105
14 COMMIT TO FAITHFUL PERSONS 117
15 "QUITE A LION" IN AMERICA......................127
16 WINDS OF REVIVAL BLOW SOUTH 133
17 MADE PERFECT IN WEAKNESS 139
18 THE AFTERWARD OF HEALING 151
19 PERSONAL TESTIMONY 161
20 DEEPER INTO SECRETS...........................177
21 MISSIONARY STATESMAN 187
22 POWER FOR OUTREACH 195
23 AN ANOINTED PEN 205
24 RIPENING YEARS — CLIMBING HIGHER 221
25 THE FAMILY TOUCH..............................237
26 NOT SUNSET BUT PROMOTION 245

APPENDIX
BIBLIOGRAPHY

PREFACE

"It is wonderful how the written page can give back the spirit of a man with all its heroic influences." Andrew Murray wrote the above words about *another* man's biography. If I have been able even to approach this high goal by providing new generations of readers with a living, human, flesh-and-blood Andrew Murray, I will be satisfied.

The books of this spiritual giant of yesterday have influenced my own Christian life since I was in my teens. I could hardly understand their spiritual heights in my immaturity, but instinctively I knew that this man of God beckoned me to start climbing a mountain that would take a lifetime to scale. Through my years of academic preparation, then ministry for the Lord on the mission field and in varied types of Christian service, I read Murray's books over and over, underlining new sentences which leaped into my spiritual horizon of need. I wrote dozens of poems sparked by phrases from his writings which spoke intensely to my spirit. I feel that I was nourished and sustained on Murray's soundly Biblical teachings and drawn to launch out into the deep with God.

But I always wanted to know *the man behind the words.* Was he real? Was he "of like passions"? What happened in his life to cause him to write with such deep conviction on certain themes? Did he laugh or was he always stern? Was he approachable? What was his family like? Did he always talk in "thees" and "thous"? Did he live on a pedestal or rub shoulders with ordinary people? Was he always "on top of it" in spiritual victory, or did he struggle and sometimes become discouraged like me?

A contemporary biography of Andrew Murray is long overdue. His biographies are out of print and to be found only in libraries. But there is a fullness of time — this is the appropriate year for a new biography to be published — the 150th anniversary of his birth in 1828.

I admit to feeling a keen sense of destiny, certainly mingled with unworthiness, as if chosen by God (and with a nod of approval from Andrew himself!) to write this new biography. To have researched his life was a holy task. I will never be the same. I experienced a spiritual high even while digging into otherwise tedious archives of research. In a condensed span of time, I lived vicariously through Murray's life from his ancestral roots to his last breath of praise as he finally beheld the Lord whom he loved with such fervor.

I laughed and I cried as I experienced tender and traumatic episodes of his life with him. I became spiritually richer in becoming so well acquainted with him. I have called him "Andrew" throughout the book because I knew him from boyhood — and so will you, as you read the book.

For the rest of my life, as I read his books with the fresh understanding of the very human Andrew Murray, what he has written will enter more deeply into my heart. I know now that he walked the roads that I walk. He speaks to my struggles in the flesh and to my triumphs in the Spirit. I can think of him only in the present tense, and talk about him to my friends in that way. I actually think I'll recognize him one day in Glory when I meet him as part of the "communion of saints" from all ages.

I hope you'll feel the same way when you finish this book!

PORTRAIT BY PEN

If you had an opportunity to meet Andrew Murray in person, in the prime of his ministry — if you could shake his hand, have some private conversation with him, and then sit under his preaching as part of an audience numbering into the thousands, how would he impress you? How would you describe him physically and by manner?

A treasured insight is provided for us by the late Rev. H. V. Taylor which appeared in the *British Weekly* newspaper on December 6, 1894. The occasion was one of Andrew's visits to England, America, and Europe for conference ministry.

Let us meet Andrew Murray through the eyes of a firsthand observer:

The title of catholic . . . is most appropriate for this man of wide sympathies and love. "We are *Christian first* and Dutch Reformed afterward," he declared while addressing Synod delegates from many different churches of his denomination. This statement gives the keynote of his life.

Mr. Murray desires to be known as a Christian, simply as a follower of Jesus. He seems to examine everyone he meets for the Christian element in him. This is the impression left on the mind when one is in conversation with him. His keen, yearning look scans the face of the one with whom he is speaking to see if the witness of the Christ-life is there, and to plead, above all things, for loyalty to his Master. You cannot help saying to yourself, "This man wants *me* to belong to Jesus Christ." No one who has talked with him, even on casual themes, can forget that wistful glance.

His nature is profoundly devotional; he carries with him the atmosphere of prayer. He seems always wrapped about with a mantle of adoration. When preaching or conducting a service, his whole being is thrown into the task and he glows with a fervency of spirit which it seems impossible for human flesh to sustain.

At times he startles and overwhelms listeners. Earnestness and power of the electric sort stream from him and affect the large audience in the same way as the quiet circle gathered around him.

In his slight, spent frame of middle height, he carries in repose a volcanic energy which, when he is roused, bursts its barriers and sweeps all before it. Then his form quivers and dilates, his lips tremble, his features work, his eyes spasmodically open and close, as from the white-hot furnace of his spirit he pours the molten torrent of his unstudied eloquence. The thin face and almost emaciated body are transfigured and illumined.

The staid, venerable minister of the nineteenth century, with the sober, clerical garb and stiff white tie, which is *de rigueur* among the Dutch clergy, disappears and an old Hebrew prophet stands before us — another Isaiah with his glowing imagery, a second Hosea with his plaintive, yearning appeals.

Audiences bend before the sweeping rain of his words like willows before a gale. The heart within the hearer is bowed, and the intellect awed. Andrew Murray's oratory is of that kind for which men willingly go into captivity.

His disposition is mystical. As in the best of mystics, the religious thought clothes a strong and fearless nature. No man can study his face without being struck by the inwardness of the deep-set grey eyes. Even when one gets to hand-grips with him in closeness of company, one is conscious of the great part that remains unexpressed, the spiritual *hinterland* which extends far beyond the visible shore. There is always the suggestion of great strength held in reserve.

A student of character cannot help being convinced that if the old days of persecution were to return, *Andrew Murray would go to the stake as cheerfully as he steps up to the Moderator's chair!*

INTRODUCTION

"Why hath the Lord put me in the ministry — unfit as I am — leaving me to wrestle with the awful work in my own impotency? Oh! Why can I not find the needful strength?" lamented the young Andrew Murray, fresh from seminary.

HERE WAS A MAN — a discouraged minister of barely twenty-five years, struggling with his lack of spiritual power. But he was destined to become one of the best loved and most widely read writers on the deeper Christian life. In his eighty-eight years he wrote about 240 books and tracts which were published in fifteen languages. Many of his works are being republished eagerly today. He had an anointed pen because he had an anointed heart. He did indeed find that power from God for which he had hungered, found it in the full blessing of Pentecost in his personal life and ministry.

HERE WAS A MAN who, since childhood, had heard his minister-father plead and pray with tears of anguish for revival, in which prayers Andrew joined, yet who did not recognize immediately the outpouring of the Holy Spirit when it was happening in his own congregation. In fact, he sought to stop it — but was inundated with the Spirit himself, resulting in the transformation of his ministry.

HERE WAS A MAN who was too early famous, a boy preacher to whose meetings admiring crowds flocked, who could count conversions at every evangelistic service — and who fought the insidious inroads of pride and self-esteem as his archenemies. This was the man who wrote a masterpiece on humility when God dealt deeply with him.

HERE WAS A MAN whom most people know only for his devotional writings, but who was a missionary force that shook his generation; a missionary statesman of whom churches and conventions took serious notice and who enlisted missionary candidates by the hundreds for pioneer works — giving his own sons and daughters for the missionary cause.

HERE WAS A MAN who was an educationalist, a founder of institutions for secular and religious training, upgrading the academic standard of his country and times. He was involved on every level of community and national importance to the betterment of his fellow men.

HERE WAS A MAN — a church politician, in the best sense of the word — who was a recognized leader from God in any gathering into which he stepped. Not all agreed with him, but his advice was sought, his wishes respected; and his opinions counted with people of all ages and every degree of social standing. It was not because he was an authoritarian figure, but because he was known as being in constant touch with God. Six times elected Moderator of the Synod of the Dutch Reformed Church in South Africa, he defended the Faith in civil courts in his country and left a permanent mark on the denomination with which he served.

HERE WAS A MAN who worked for spiritual renewal within the established church and who reaped the results of his prayers and labors in a deep moving of the Holy Spirit in his generation.

HERE WAS A MAN — a family man, a tender, loving husband and devoted father of eight children — who had a special rapport with youngsters all his life. He was always involved with youth, molding young seminarians who lived in his home into godly characters and shaping their destinies. He was a man of laughter and humor and ready wit for appropriate occasions.

HERE WAS A MAN whose spirit ripened in maturing years to a full golden harvest in the setting sun — who lost no spiritual zest or optimism as his outer man grew more frail. He stepped over the final earthly line separating our "now" from eternity with an eager anticipation and genuine joy.

HERE WAS A MAN who was "not a voice alone, but a force; who created not merely an influence, but an atmosphere for God." There were few in his land and generation who had not either heard him preach or met him in person.

We, too, have an opportunity to MEET THIS MAN — Andrew Murray — in the pages that follow.

Of course, he had to start out as a winsome, rollicking, little Scottish boy . . .

1

Sailing Toward New Horizons

"Goodbye! Goodbye, dear Mamma, Papa! See you soon!"

The lad of ten years, outfitted in an adult-styled black suit with starched shirt and ruffled cuffs, grabbed for his brimmed stiff hat with one hand and waved frantically to his parents with the other. The wind whipped the words from his lips as the ship unfurled its sails and slipped away from the pier. He clung to the rail, swaying with the strange and uncomfortable ocean surge.

"Andrew, you shouldn't say 'soon' — you know we will be away for a long, long time," solemnly corrected his brother, John. All of two inches taller and two years older, similarly clad in Sunday finery, the elder of the Murray brothers steadied himself and also continued to wave. Their voices could no longer be heard over the noise of the flapping sails and squeaks of the rings and rigging-ropes against the masts.

Turning to his young brother, John saw large tears trickling down Andrew's pale face. The boy had held them back bravely during the whole scene at Port

Elizabeth, South Africa, while taking leave of their father and mother and other relatives. Now he could restrain himself no longer. He did not cry aloud but gently sobbed, biting his lip for control.

John put his arm awkwardly around the boy. "Andrew, God will always be with us. And He will be with Papa and Mamma back there, too, and with William, Maria, Charles and baby Jemima. Just think," he tried diverting Andrew with small talk, "Jemima will be as old as I am right now when we get back!"

Andrew giggled and stifled a sob at the same time in such a way that both boys burst out laughing. "Come now, we must go down to the cabins. It is getting cold in the wind even though it's sunny. It will soon be time to eat."

The year was 1838 and the two elder sons of the Rev. Andrew Murray, Sr. had set sail in July for Scotland in the care of fellow passengers Rev. and Mrs. James Archbell, Wesleyan missionaries who were homeward bound on furlough. It had been arranged for the boys to live at their uncle's home in Aberdeen, Scotland, to pursue their education.

The voyage was a miserable one that did not land them at their destination until well into autumn. Questioned in later years as to what he remembered about the trip, Andrew candidly remarked, "Nothing at all except that Mrs. Archbell had a baby." It is fortunate that memories fade with time, for the lad arrived in Scotland suffering from scurvy and not in the best of health from prolonged seasickness, limited nutrition, and change of climate. Used to sunny South Africa, the Murray boys found it difficult to adjust to bleak and wintry Scotland. Doubtless they did not fully grasp the length of time it was proposed that they should remain away — another duplicate life span of Andrew's ten years. It is the Lord's mercy to veil for us the time required to reach the distant goal and allow us to concern ourselves with one step at a time.

That first step for Andrew and John upon arrival in Scotland was to be enrolled in school the very next day after they set foot on non-swaying land. Uncle John, their father's minister-brother, was a respected, conservative, strict but loving disciplinarian who didn't believe that time should be wasted. He was one of the keenest of the evangelical clergymen of his country, a serious scholar, and a deeply spiritual man. He had influenced his brother, Andrew Murray, Sr., in much the same way as young John was to influence his brother Andrew with godly guidance and caring companionship. Andrew Murray, Sr. had the utmost confidence to commit his sons to the care of his brother's family, which consisted of uncle, aunt, one son and three daughters of about the same age as the Murray family in South Africa. It turned out to be a most happy, though difficult, seven years of preparation, which left a lasting impression on every area of the boys' lives.

But how did it happen that one Scottish Murray brother, Andrew, Sr., was planted in a Dutch community in South Africa and the other Murray brother, John, remained in the land of their birth, both serving as ministers? And why were the sons of the South African Murray seeking their education so far away in the land of their father's birth? God's ways are mysterious but perfect.

In His sovereignty, God had planned for South Africa to produce a son who would influence for Jesus

Christ, through his preaching and writing, not only the land of his birth, but Europe and America, and the people of many nations for generations to come. It was this very lad of ten, the young Andrew Murray, born on May 9, 1828, who was destined by God to speak to coming generations as few men have been privileged to do. His name has become a household word in Christian homes and churches throughout the world through his 240 books and tracts in English and Dutch. His works have been published in more than fifteen languages.

Deep Roots for Strong Trees

The ancestors of the Murrays were associated with the Presbyterian Church of Scotland, a godly heritage. The immediate ancestors of Andrew Murray, Sr., the father of our subject, were farmers in Aberdeenshire, Scotland. Both his father and grandfather bore the given name of Andrew.

Andrew, Sr.'s father died while comparatively young, and on his deathbed he prayed aloud for his four children by name. John, one of the two boys, only twelve at the time, overheard his father's prayer and the impression made on him was so deep that he dedicated himself to the service of Christ, resolving to educate himself for the ministry and also to assist his brother Andrew in his education. This he did indeed, with the help of Almighty God.

History was repeating itself in 1838 with another set of brothers with the same names, the elder looking after the younger.

The favorite son of his widowed mother, Andrew, Sr. had warmly returned the affection of his mother, a woman of great beauty and loveableness. He tried to obey her wishes in all matters. At the close of his college course he received an invitation to St. John's parish in Newfoundland, but refused in order to remain near his mother.

But when another call came, which he recognized to be from God, he felt strongly that he must accept it. In spite of his tender love for his mother, he left her while she lay on what proved to be her deathbed, without letting her know what a far place he was setting out for. The ultimate destination was South Africa, considered the most remote corner of the world in those days.

As he waited for the stagecoach which was to take him away, he and his brother John committed one another to God's care and sang together the old hymn "O God of Bethel," which became the family hymn in the widely scattered Murray households. They were never to see one another again, but Andrew, Sr.'s sons were to live their formative years under their uncle's roof. Andrew, Sr. studied Dutch in Holland for several months and then sailed for South Africa.

What prompted this strong call to the young Scotsman to cause him to choose it above prestigious pulpits in his fatherland? In 1652 the Dutch East India Company had founded a settlement at the Cape of Good Hope without planning to colonize the country; it was only to be a convenient port of call between Holland and the East, a place to refresh the crews and obtain supplies. But as the population increased, the sturdy Dutchmen ignored the company's policy and formed settlements inland, seeking better living conditions. Devout men, they established congregations in those scattered communities and a virile Dutch Church took shape along patterns of the church in Holland. It also depended upon its supply of ministers from there.

After the British arrived in the early 1800's, supply of the pulpits became even more difficult, compounded by the vast distances between the congregations. From the beginning, the Dutch Church was closely connected with the government; this situation persisted even after the coming of the British. In all respects it was the national church of the country. The Governor of the Cape, Lord Henry Somerset, requested the Rev. Dr. George Thom, who had come to South Africa in connection with the London Missionary Society, but was the minister of the Dutch Church of Caledon, to try to obtain a supply of ministers from Scotland.

It was Andrew Murray, Sr. who, in 1821, responded to his recruitment, the first of a number of able Scotsmen who heard the Macedonian cry for help and left their homeland for permanent ministry in Africa. Andrew Murray, Sr.'s appointment upon arrival was to the district of Graaff-Reinet.

There was a significant oneness between the two great Presbyterian Churches, that of Scotland and the Dutch Reformed Church of South Africa — the only difference being one of language, which Murray, Sr. soon surmounted. He learned to preach fluently in Dutch.

In his early thirties, Rev. Murray still lacked something very important to his ministry — a wife. In Cape Town, on a trip related to a synod meeting, he met a beautiful young lady, Maria Stegmann, who married him the following year when she was only sixteen. She was less than twenty when young Andrew, the subject of our story, was born. His mother's combined German, French Huguenot and Calvinist Dutch ancestry mingled with his father's pure Scottish blood to give Andrew a sturdy heritage.

Andrew, Sr. so identified with the land of his adoption that his children could never remember hearing him express any longing even to visit Scotland. His parish, Graaff-Reinet, in which young Andrew spent the first ten years of his life, was and still is one of the most important towns in the Cape province. The congregation was founded in 1790, and for almost ninety years some member of the Murray family served the pulpit. Andrew, Sr.'s pastorate extended over 44 years. Graaff-Reinet is on a well-watered plain situated in the midst of the dry tableland called the Karroo, about 500 miles northeast of Cape Town and 140 miles north of Port Elizabeth.

Young Andrew's boyhood was a happy but disciplined one. The children were well trained in the ways of the Lord and obeyed their father unquestionably; his word was law; from his decision there was no appeal; his wisdom was never debated. This attitude was evident during the years of absence abroad of his two sons, who consulted their father through correspondence and assented to his every decision. It was a loving, willing obedience, by no means forced.

Father Murray's conversations with his children were always purposeful; on rides into the countryside he would instruct them about natural history or geography or other matters of the world. He made a point to speak to each of his children concerning their spiritual condition on appropriate occasions. Sometimes it was on Sunday evenings after family worship when the children came to him for a good-night kiss.

The elder children were expected to be concerned for the spiritual affairs of the younger. Singing of hymns and memorization of Scripture were indelibly imprinted on the Murray children's memories.

Nor did Andrew forget his father's sacred Friday evening habit: he regularly devoted the whole time praying for revival. He would shut himself in his study and read accounts of former revivals in Scotland and other countries and often read stories to the family of the outpouring of the Holy Spirit on some particular church. Andrew vividly remembered standing outside the study door listening to his father's loud crying to God and pleading for a similar outpouring in his own parish, elsewhere in South Africa, and in the world.

Andrew, Sr. lived to see some answers. At a conference in Worcester in 1860, when the wave of blessing which had swept over America, Ireland, Scotland, and England had just reached the shores of Africa, he quite broke down before the gathering when he spoke of his great longing for revival. Within a year the blessing came to his own congregation.

Long before slavery was abolished, Andrew, Sr. had aligned himself with the cause of the slaves. In his own household he would not allow any service by a black person without first giving the individual his or her liberty and providing fair treatment and a good living standard.

Because Andrew's mother was so young, she was a close companion to her sons and daughters. She was known as a contented person, thoroughly happy in her husband, in her children, and supremely happy in the love of God. Rest and peace in the midst of much work was her hallmark. Communion with God was the secret.

Children and servants knew that mother must not be disturbed when she shut her door for private devotions. She became the mother of eleven children, most of them becoming ministers or marrying ministers, and thus exerting a wide influence for Christ.

The Murray home was a crossroads for important persons in the Christian world because Graaff-Reinet was on the main road to the interior. The parsonage provided hospitality to many of the remarkable missionaries of those early days: Dr. Moffat and Dr. Livingstone, the earlier French missionaries, and many from Scotland and Germany. The Murray manse was spacious, on two levels, in every respect the finest residence in the village, finer than the house of the magistrate. It had a huge yard and outbuildings, with a large garden of flowers, a vineyard and fruit trees. Indoors was an immense dining hall, drawing rooms, study, many bedrooms, connecting rooms with arches — all a delight for the children to play hide-and-seek with playmates, who were always welcome. The house habitually resounded with merriment, even as a parsonage. All was dedicated to the Lord, a haven to friend or stranger for physical and spiritual refreshment.

From such a large and godly family and church environment, young Andrew was severed at the tender age of ten. A sensitive boy, he was described as "exuberant in spirit, less quiet than his brother in thought and speech, of a retentive memory and able easily to assimilate knowledge; not less earnest than his brother and devout from childhood." The two brothers who were to be close companions for all their formative years were in many respects a contrast: John favoring his father — silent, reserved, and cautious in word and act; Andrew favoring his mother in his features and character, with bright and eager disposition.

The boys had a loyal affection for each other without jealousy or competitiveness. John frankly admired the talents of Andrew who, although two years younger, kept up with him all through their studies. And Andrew revered John's steadiness of character and sober judgment. He tried hard to imitate John's diligence and his good work habits.

Why was it necessary for the Murray boys to leave such an ideal environment? It was not common to send children abroad in the early 1800's, the distance to Europe being so great, with no convenience of "flying home for vacation breaks." But public education at that period in South Africa was at its lowest ebb, because poor salaries did not attract high quality teachers. Little more than the three R's were taught. Enterprising parents in some of the larger towns pooled their resources and tried hiring a teacher who would at least instruct in Latin and mathematics. The Senior Murrays were genuinely concerned about the education of their two elder sons who showed great academic promise. After much thought and prayer, the parents decided to send their sons to Scotland. The separation was not easy for parents or children, but the youngsters proved mature enough to understand that it was for their highest welfare and was motivated by the love of their parents.

That Andrew did see the difficult separation in the proper perspective and reverenced and loved his parents for it, and appreciated the foundation of love and spiritual nurture they had already invested in him, is reflected in a memo to the entire Murray family circle when he had reached an advanced age:

A godly parentage is a priceless boon. Its blessings rest not only upon the children of the first generation, but have often been traced in many successive generations. But its blessings will depend upon the keeping up of the spirit of prayer, with that direct sense of belonging to God. When God blessed Abraham and his seed it was that through them all the nations of the earth were to be blessed. And so God still means that a family which He blesses should be the channel through which a neighborhood or a people shall learn to know Him.

To belong to such a family implies high privilege, but equally high responsibility. The spirit of the world is so strong, the slackening of the spiritual life on the part of the parents comes in so easily, that unless the charge God has committed to us be jealously guarded, the inheritance may easily become spent and lost. It is well for a family to acknowledge what it owes to the prayers of its ancestors.

Sturdy Branches Spread

For all practical purposes, young Andrew and John were adopted into a new family for seven years. After having a happy and contented Mamma as their home's guiding light in Africa, they found their aunt a contrast in temperament. Often depressed and moody, without a buoyant spirit, she was nevertheless treated tenderly by Uncle John Murray who stood by her with comfort in her times of difficulty. To observe firsthand such a patient spirit in his saintly uncle caused Andrew in later years to write understandingly and with sympathy toward doubting and unsettled Christians.

A tribute to the boys' behavior under all circumstances was given by one of their cousins. "Their uncle and aunt never once had to find fault with either of the boys during their entire stay in our home. We, the younger members of the family, counted them as brothers and were brokenhearted when they left us."

The boys were sure their parents were praying for them continually and trusting them to do their best, so they applied themselves well to their studies. They had another incentive: the local lads and lassies had the distorted idea that anyone who came from Africa must be an utter savage, which included lads of the Colonies. Andrew and John took it upon themselves to prove that this was not so. They soon earned the respect of their peers through their ability in the main subject of the grammar school, Latin. Although the Murray boys had received no instruction in Latin other than that given by their father, what they had acquired was equal to that of the local students.

As the boys advanced into their teens and took the entrance exams at Marischal College, it was Andrew, then only thirteen, who qualified for a scholarship. The boys continued on the same grade level throughout their academic preparation.

Their father lovingly and seriously kept close tab on his boys through letters, and they reciprocated with a great deal of correspondence which has been preserved.

"My dear boys," wrote the Senior Murray, "you may both depend on it, though you are out of our sight you are seldom out of mind. We always follow you with our fervent prayers. . . . I trust you will ever remember that our having sent you abroad for study was for your own good. Had my affection for you swayed me to keep you here, you could never have seen or known the half of the good you are likely to see and know now. It will, however, under the blessing of God, depend much on yourselves whether or not the step we have taken shall be for your real benefit in this life and that which is to come."

He salted his letters with practical advice: "Try to keep as far up in your classes as you possibly can. Do your homework in the evenings and don't count on the morning hours before school too much. . . . Write often, everything about yourselves, your friends, your lodgings and studies. It will all be interesting to us and your friends and relatives here at home." With no air-mail facility, letters back and forth took many months, as did the parcels which passed frequently between them.

One letter was held up temporarily by Andrew: ".... We delayed answering your letter, dear Papa and Mamma, because we wanted to see what our success might be at the end of the term. That success, however, has been very small. John has gotten *seventh* prize in Mathematics!" But both boys did exceptionally well and received their share of honors and prizes during the seven years.

While the boys were in Aberdeen, the Free Church of Scotland came into being in 1843, when fully a third of those in the Scottish state church pulled out. Thomas Chalmers, R. M. McCheyne and, in particular, the revivalist preacher W. C. Burns (who became a missionary to China in 1847) were largely responsible for the disruption.

At the same time, the religious climate in Scotland was verging on revival. Philanthropy, education, and religion were all claiming fresh attention; politically, the Chartists were active. Under the inspiration of the great-hearted and saintly Dr. Thomas Chalmers, everything evangelical received a new impulse. Recognized as the greatest preacher of his time, attracting great crowds, to the salvation of many, his influence on the church was powerful. He did not emphasize structural church planting as much as he did outreach with the Word: carrying the gospel to homes through visitation and witness.

Solid views regarding the inspiration of the Scriptures as the sole and supreme authority and rule of faith and morals also came to the fore at this time. Among the younger evangelicals were Dr. Candlish, Robert Murray McCheyne, the two Bonars, and A. N. Somerville. John and Andrew undoubtedly were present at the meetings of many of these godly men, especially in the great tent gatherings and mass meetings at which Dr. Chalmers preached to crowds of 6,000 to 10,000 people, by whom he was fully heard — without a P.A. system!

It was Andrew's assignment to read aloud to his Uncle John while the latter had his dinner, and by this wise arrangement many a thought from these great preachers was sown in the fertile soil of his keen young mind which would bear a harvest in his own preaching and writing in later years.

A great spiritual awakening was passing over Scotland similar to that which had stirred America under Charles Finney. The man God used to implement it was the young Rev. William C. Burns, who was destined to have a great influence over both the lads, but especially over Andrew. Mr. Burns was described as "inexperienced, with slow speech, no particular gifts of charm or eloquence or winning sweetness. But he had about him such an air of divine commission that he could not be criticized and drew even careless people to receive him as a messenger of God." His few, plain words were full of weight and power, finding their mark directly in men's hearts because he spent much time in prayer and fasting. He was particularly effective in youth ministry.

Mr. Burns was often a guest in Uncle John's home,

having been taught the Word by him in his early years, so Andrew and John came into close touch with him. Andrew even had the dubious honor, at age twelve, to carry Mr. Burns' coat and Bible to church, which seems to have been some kind of coveted privilege. What Andrew saw of this man's genuine spiritual life, power with God, and public ministry, affected him deeply.

On one occasion after Mr. Burns had left, he answered a letter that young John wrote him. He used strong but loving words to warn him. "You are not excusable in remaining in your present unrenewed state. There really is not the smallest possible hope of your being saved unless you are really born of the Holy Spirit and reconciled to the Holy Jehovah by the atoning blood of His only begotten Son. Search your heart, my dear fellow-sinner.... Oh, dear friend, be not tempted to put off to a more convenient season your entire consecration to Emmanuel. . . ."

He added a P.S. "Show this to Andrew to whom it may also apply. I'll answer his letter later."

Toward the end of their studies in Scotland, the boys were advised by their father to begin serious thought and prayer about the choice of their life vocations. He advised them not to take up some career which they could just as well have trained for by remaining in South Africa. That would have defeated the purpose of being sent abroad for wider opportunities of study.

"I do hope you won't think of law, because our Bench and Bar here are corrupt. Should you feel inclined toward theology or medicine or business, I have no doubt there will always be openings at the Cape as well as at other places. If I were you, I'd at least be open to consider the Indian Missions — *there* is something worthy of the ambition of great minds. Even to enter education would be worthy. . . ."

Andrew's letter to his father must have crossed in the mail. In it he had already informed his father that, after careful thought and prayer, he had decided to give himself to the work of preaching the gospel.

His father answered, ". . . I have now to congratulate you on your choice of a profession and rejoice that the Lord has been pleased to incline your heart the way He has done." Then he added a serious comment, "I trust, however, my dear boy, that you have given your heart to Jesus Christ, to be His now and His forever, to follow Him through good and through bad report."

It appears that not infrequently in those days, when the service of the Church was such a viable career choice, and pursued by so many, that young men often entered the ministry without having been born again. And the line between being brought up in a devout Christian environment, accepting Christianity as a matter of fact, as against a definite, personal decision of repentance and crisis of new birth, was a very indistinct line for some. The caution was not misplaced, because young Andrew did, indeed, date his personal conversion several years later; it was perceptive of his father to draw this distinction.

The elder Murray went on to counsel his son: "The service in the Church in South Africa does not promise you much wealth or ease in this world, but a field of usefulness as extensive as you could desire among a kind and indulgent people. . . . I would recommend that you study divinity a year or two in the Free Church of Scotland, and then go for a year or two to Holland, as much for the Dutch language as for theology, and get licensed and ordained for the Church at the Cape."

The more reflective brother, John, seems to have taken longer to reach his decision to become a minister. His problem was mainly that he regarded the claims of the ministry as too exalted for his devotion and strength. After some indecision, and strong counsel from his Uncle John, to whom he was closer than was Andrew, he too determined to devote himself to theology.

In the spring of 1845 the brothers simultaneously passed their final exams in the arts and graduated with an M.A. from Marischal College, Andrew being not quite seventeen. The next step was to take the theological course in Holland, which was to require three more years of study in God's classroom of preparation for their life ministries.

Chocolate Club and Long Gouda Pipes

"When I went to Holland, they overcharged me because I didn't speak Dutch," warned Andrew's father in a letter before the boys left Scotland. "And watch out for their abominable customs of drinking gin and water and smoking tobacco and cigars. Entertain your friends with tea and coffee — Holland is famous for both. Don't be afraid to be different."

Their father went on to advise against theological teachings which were not based on the Bible. "Be sure not to neglect your daily study of the Holy Scriptures. . .; pray much for the guidance of the Holy Spirit."

The Murray brothers set sail from Scotland in June, 1845, to enroll at the Academy of Utrecht, which later became the State University. Because they arrived shortly before the beginning of summer vacation, they had time to get used to an alien environment. They could speak only English and very imperfect Dutch, so they attempted to get along in the student circles with Latin.

One of their new friends commented that upon first sight he did not know what to make of them: "There were two youths in somewhat strange garb walking along the streets with cheerful countenances and unassuming demeanor . . . and whether their Latin was classically pure, or even intelligible or endurable, is open to question. But it was sufficient and we understood one another."

The boys had the immediate good fortune to get in with a unique group of fellow Christian students; the religious condition of Holland at that time was deplorable. Rationalism from Germany was spreading, and pulpits were occupied by ministers who had no use for evangelical doctrine, even though by form they were still bound to preach the Calvinistic theology of the Dutch Reformed Church. The Christian lives of laymen were weak, and most held only to a diluted form of Sunday religion. Conversion was an antiquated word and the Holy Spirit appeared to have been replaced by the spirit of the times. Strange views of "broadminded" men were the order of the day. The professors and the courses to which the Murrays were exposed reflected the religious corruption. It was said of the theological professors that their lectures "tasted of long Gouda pipes." What a climate in which to nurture two young men who were to influence their generation significantly for the evangelical faith!

One spiritual spark, however, leaped over from Switzerland and ignited some Christians in Holland who were hoping and praying for "seasons of refreshing from the presence of the Lord." The spiritual condition of Switzerland was even worse, if possible, than Holland. Two Scottish laymen, Robert and James Haldane, burdened with the deadness of a church that had been founded by Calvin, embarked on an evangelistic mission to Switzerland and started Bible readings for the theological students at Geneva. Through some of their converts and co-workers, their influence penetrated Holland and became known by its French name *Réveil*, or Revival. It did not originate in church circles, but in literary circles, being largely confined to the aristocratic and upper middle classes. Influenced by the Réveil, in 1843 some Christian students at Utrecht founded the society known as Zekor Dabar ("Remember the Word," in Hebrew) "to promote the study of the subjects required for the ministerial calling in the spirit of the Revival." This was the group that gave a warm welcome to the Murrays.

The meetings of the society were held once a week in rotation in the rooms of each member, who would serve as host. The study and discussion of theological subjects took up the first three hours, at nine o'clock extemporaneous orations were heard, ending at ten when simple refreshments of bread, butter, cheeses and beverage were enjoyed with open fellowship. It was the refreshments that labeled them from the outside in a derogatory way. Because the group avoided wine and liquor and drank only coffee, tea, and Dutch chocolate, they were dubbed the "Chocolate Club." Members were ridiculed by professors as too fanatical; fellow students refused to sit by these "pious fellows" in class or to rub shoulders with them in the halls.

No hermit clique, the group spent much time in gospel outreach. They held makeshift Sunday Schools for poor children, Bible classes for working men, and instead of enjoying their own recreation time, the young men devoted it to visiting the poor and preaching the gospel. With a vision beyond their immediate locale, the society and the Murrays pioneered a missionary band which met twice a month to pray for and learn about missions. The group began to publish its own sixteen-page monthly mission magazine in Dutch during the time the Murrays studied in Holland.

There is a striking similarity between the Murray brothers and two other brothers more than a hundred years earlier. Another famous circle of young men met in one of the rooms of Lincoln College, Oxford, England, whose leaders were John and Charles Wesley. Although the results of the two groups were different, they shared the same spirit of intense earnestness, enthusiasm to live consistent Christian lives, to align doctrine and living, and to reach out in good works. And both groups encountered ridicule and persecution from fellow students.

To study in such an adverse religious environment can destroy the faith of some Christian students even in our day. But it can also have the opposite effect, to strengthen it, which was the case with the Murrays. The new intellectual atmosphere to which they were introduced and the conflict with well-educated people who took different theological views, caused them to examine their own foundations of faith in Christ more closely and come out stronger by recommitting themselves to their heritage of faith in the Bible.

It was at Utrecht in 1845, when Andrew was only seventeen, that he experienced a great change in his life which he himself called his conversion. This despite the fact that he was already assured of God's call to enter the ministry as a vocation and had been sincerely committed to Christian matters from his childhood. To him this conversion was a distinct event which he could date and pinpoint in location to the very house and room. It was no cataclysmic experience of the moment, but a precise time of complete surrender to Christ from which he dated a new era of his life. This milestone launched his whole ministry and set his sights for scores of years serving his Lord.

Andrew's own words describe it in a letter of congratulations to his parents after he found out that a new child, another son, had been born to his parents:

"... And equal, I am sure, will be your delight when I tell you that I can communicate to you far gladder tidings, over which angels have rejoiced, that your son has been born again. In my previous letters and conversation you may have noted a stiffness in my speaking about such things, and even now I hardly know how to write.... For the last several years there has been a continual process in my spiritual life. It did bother me and held me back that I lacked some kind of deep sight of my sins, which many other people seemed to have, before I could be converted. At present I can say that I am confident that as a sinner I have cast myself on Christ.... Dear Parents, praise the Lord with me.... I am peaceful and have a true confidence in God though my feelings of joy and prayer are not always consistent. My heart at present is warm, yet whenever I begin to write or speak, I fail.... I have a long way to go before I can do nothing but praise Him fully and continually.... Oh, that I might receive grace to walk more holy before Him!"

The tone of his letters to his parents noticeably changed to continual praise and genuine enthusiasm for Christ and his personal part in God's work. In writing of the missionary prayer meeting of the Chocolate Club,

Andrew refers to their interceding, together with Christians everywhere, "for the outpouring of God's Spirit on the world." He began to consider further theological education in Germany after his Holland studies because "the lectures here are such that it is almost impossible to get any good from them." Besides, he reasoned via letters to his father, he would be only twenty years old at his graduation and that was under age for ordination. "And the living standard is cheaper in Germany," he added as an incentive. As much as Andrew longed to do this, he submitted himself to his father's wisdom whether both he and John should return to Africa after graduation.

The answer came back from Papa that although Andrew could probably not be ordained before the age of twenty-two, there would be plenty of openings for usefulness to the Lord after his return, and it would be better for Andrew to get some experience before he had the full responsibility of a congregation. In fact, he hinted of "mission type" challenges right within South Africa which should appeal to any earnest young Christian worker.

Andrew replied that his full desire was to place himself in God's hands to be used wherever God chose, even if it was to return immediately to Africa and forego more European education. "Because" — Andrew was good at rationalizing — "an additional stock of human wisdom often proves nothing else than obstruction in God's way." At the same time, Andrew confessed that it was one of his natural weaknesses to be quite nonchalant about God's leading, with a certain indifference and contentedness as to the future, rather than having a strong, active burden of concern for God's work. But the zeal and burden that he felt he lacked came more completely with maturity and Andrew's full baptism in the Holy Spirit in later years.

During one of their long vacations, the Murrays set off on an enjoyable walking tour of the Rhine Valley where they met a Pastor Blumhardt; they were exposed for the first time to a remarkable work for the demon possessed and healing of the sick by faith. This movement was to lead into a great revival in the Rhenish provinces. Seeing for himself the reality of God's continuing miracles, Andrew's convictions about the validity of the power of God being available even today were firmly established. He wrote with firsthand knowledge and conviction in these areas in later years.

Prayer and intercession were prominent themes in Andrew's writings in his maturity. His experience was based on his own appreciation of the prayers of his parents for himself and his brother while they were separated for ten years. In his books about godly child training, this spirit is likewise reflected. He wrote to his parents, "I am sure we have often reaped the fruits of your believing prayers even while we were still unacquainted with true prayer. I trust we may still go on to experience what a blessing praying parents are. . . . May God grant you a rich answer to the many prayers you have offered for us by abundantly blessing your own souls."

On Andrew's twentieth birthday, May 9, 1848, The Hague Committee broke precedent and ordained both John and Andrew. The farewell gathering for the Murray boys was a deeply emotional affair for the Chocolate Club, with Bible readings, extended prayers, singing, and celebrating holy communion together. The group crowded around them singing Psalm 134, weeping and embracing the brothers whom they had grown to love so dearly. John pronounced the benediction, and at half past ten the boys climbed into a waiting carriage which was to take them to Vreeswijk and the voyage home.

The Murrays made a farewell visit to their uncle's home in Aberdeen and the two boys were given the honor of preaching in his church. The family and congregation, who knew them from their arrival as scarcely more than children, had a hard time to decide "which of the twa laddies was the grander preacher."

Andrew's preparation in Holland was a deeply significant period in his life. He formed habits of self-evaluation in those student years which developed his gracious Christian character and his fruitful ministry. His broad theological and social contacts, as well as the continued companionship of his serious brother, left him with a legacy of mature judgment and thoughtful temperament.

Andrew was known for his exuberant spirits as a young man and his more conservative older brother often scolded him, "Andrew, you shouldn't laugh so much — that's not good," no doubt reflecting the spirit of their times, that religion and joy should not be joined. In Andrew's later writings, however, they were not only linked but wedded.

5

Under the Wing
of Mother Church

At last — home in South Africa after ten years! The Murray boys left as children and their return as two young ministers from Europe was an event of more than local importance. It was announced in church magazines, referred to in the newspapers, and discussed in ecclesiastical circles throughout the country.

Papa and Mamma Murray could not be at Cape Town to meet the boys, but grandparents and other relatives were on hand to enthusiastically welcome them. Young as they were, they were invited to preach in established pulpits.

The first text on which Andrew preached was, "We preach Christ crucified." "May it be true!" wrote Andrew to his parents. "But I feel it very difficult not to preach *myself*. I am afraid that I attend too much to beauty of thought and language and feel too little that God alone can teach me to preach." Andrew need not have feared, because God was just about to launch a new life-classroom experience for him in his first appointment out in the "wilderness" where his "beauty of thought and language" would count for nothing!

But first came that longed-for visit to his home at Graaff-Reinet and reunion with parents and siblings, some of whom he had never seen. Apparently Andrew's boyish and playful disposition was so outstanding that he captured the hearts of his younger brothers and sisters. "Is brother Andrew *really* a minister?" they cried. "That can never be; he's just like one of us!"

But a serious-minded minister Andrew proved to be. On the first Sunday home, the two sons of the manse shared their father's pulpit. We wonder what their feelings were. Those who heard them were deeply impressed: the younger had such an earnestness and passion; the elder had a great thoughtfulness and incisiveness. At the communion table the father and sons officiated together.

When it was Andrew's turn to serve the elements and speak briefly, he rose, closed his eyes, and seemed lost in meditation and prayer. An almost painful hush fell upon the great congregation. When he finally spoke after a long interval, the words were evidently so sincere, so intense and uplifting that tears broke out all over the assembly. Could this man of God be the same boy of ten who left for Scotland a decade ago? The deep conviction was shared by all that a destiny from God rested upon this youth to impress his generation for Christ.

The appointments for service in the church at that time were totally in the hands of the Governor of Cape Colony, Sir Harry Smith. First the interviews; then came the decisions: John was given charge of the parish at Burgerdorp, an honorable and coveted appointment. For Andrew? "I'm afraid I shall have to send you to Bloemfontein."

Thus Andrew became the pastor of a territory of nearly fifty thousand square miles, including 12,000 people, in a remote and unattractive parish beyond the Orange River. He was the first regular minister to live and work among the "voortrekkers," the hardy Dutch pioneers — backwoods people. Andrew started out on a mission field!

Comparing the size of Andrew's parish with his brother John's, someone facetiously remarked, "Since they could not place him as a minister, they made him a bishop."

Andrew Murray's life can only be fully understood with some background knowledge of the Dutch Reformed Church and its branch in South Africa. The Dutch settlement and the church were founded simultaneously in 1652, kept alive through preaching and sacraments administered by voyaging clergymen passing the Cape. During the Dutch rule, the South African church was regarded as an integral part of the church in Holland, under its control, supplied by its ministers, and paid by a paternal government. By tradition, religion was severely unemotional and chiefly a form, with little impression on the everyday life of its communicants. The church was part of the civil establishment and the ministers were government servants.

When the British rule began, theoretically the Dutch Reformed Church there was severed from its mother church in the Netherlands. But not until 1843 was a church ordinance passed which fully recognized the church's right to her own control without government interference. This was carried out with tension and difficulty, and dissatisfaction on both sides.

Thousands of farmers, Dutch Reformed Church members, were sour on British rule and in a "Great Trek" took off with their wives and children to new horizons in the territories north of the Orange River, known thereafter as the Orange Free State, the Transvaal, and Natal. Motivations were complex, not just religious. A fierce debate resulted as to whether or not the emigrants who had passed across the borders of the Colony were free from their allegiance to the British. On one side, the emigrants felt the long arm of the British reaching after them; on the other side, there were clashes with tribesmen.

One of the Cape governors in 1848 proclaimed the Queen's authority over the whole country between the Orange and Vaal rivers and annexed it under the title of the Orange River Sovereignty.

Battles of troops with emigrants followed until rebellion was at least driven underground. It was into this raw, pioneer situation that Andrew Murray plunged when he was appointed minister of Bloemfontein — the rustic pasture-capitol of the new Sovereignty.

6

Wild Dogs and Even Wilder Men

By custom, the parish which called a minister would in some manner fetch him. A huge wagon drawn by a team of powerful horses was dispatched to bring Andrew from Graaff-Reinet to his new parish, a journey of 300 miles. Accompanied by his father, all his worldly possessions, and with an escort of fifty young men on horseback, friends of Andrew, the entourage set off.

Besides his appointment as minister of Bloemfontein, Andrew was also to be acting minister of the adjoining parishes of Riet River (Fauresmith), Rietpoort (Smithfield), and Winburg. At each place the father presented his minister-son to his new congregation with an impressive ceremony. As a six-foot, slim, clean-shaven young cleric, he must have aroused many questions in the minds of seasoned, hardy, Dutch pioneers as to whether his shoulders were broad enough to carry such heavy responsibilities. Andrew had just celebrated his twenty-first birthday, and the extreme youth of this beardless boy made one old farmer exclaim: "Why, he is just a little girl!"

As the father left his young son, barely in manhood,

he took hold of the hands of the two elders and placing his son's in them, said, "Deal gently with the young man." The task which faced him was to minister Christ over a vast area, a wild country full of wild animals (lions, leopards, and vicious wild dogs) and yet wilder men — turbulent emigrants and cruel dwellers of the veld.

The distances between Andrew's outposts were great. Helicopters, Land Rovers, and four-wheel-drive jeeps were undreamed of. Most of his time was taken up in travel over all kinds of roads, in all kinds of weather, by horseback or ox wagon. The "express speed" of the latter was clocked at two miles per hour! Roads were mere tracks in the wilderness, ruts from wagons carrying merchandise from the coast to inland villages. Bridges were few and fording was more common at low points. During downpours or in the rainy season, the roads were churned to mud. Flooding rivers often made it necessary for travelers to simply wait until waters abated. Farms were few, sometimes twenty or more miles apart, with a hundred or more miles between villages.

Most outlying farmers could come to church only four times a year, when they had to travel to one of the larger villages for supplies, and so would plan their trip to coincide with the local quarterly sacramental service. On such a weekend, the minister would hold up to nine services, among them examination for confirmation of youth, marriages, baptisms, and communion services. People coming to such a center would live in their wagons or tents while loading up with enough supplies for several months.

Andrew zealously galloped his circuit, interested in the spiritual welfare not only of the privileged but also of the underprivileged. He started Sunday School classes, and Bible classes, in efforts to reach even the Hottentots and Bushmen. "We have plenty of scholars," observed Andrew, "but no teachers."

He was no believer in merely allowing his church membership candidates to go through the forms or to mouth the right answers. He insisted on thorough teaching on a long-term basis, spending many hours with the candidates person-to-person, trying to ascertain true motives for wanting to be received into the church, and the spiritual condition of each. Contrary to tradition, he rejected many "on account of their defective knowledge; others who were lacking in earnestness and had not really sought to believe in Christ."

At Bloemfontein at the communion services the number of communicants was so large that six tables had to be ministered to, each with separate hymn and address. Without a sufficiently large meeting hall, some of the gatherings took place under the open sky.

Andrew made one of his first trips through a wild dog-infested plain to reach a certain meeting about seventy miles distant. After fording a river, when he alighted from his horse to let him rest and graze, the horse suddenly caught the scent of dogs approaching and ran off. Andrew calmly took his pack on his shoulders and began a walk of about fifteen miles to the nearest house.

The surprised farmer could not believe that he had escaped the fierce dogs and arrived alive. "How did you do it?"

The calm answer was, "I knew I was in the path of duty, so I prayed to God to keep me and walked straight on. The wild dogs snapped at me but did not touch me."

Andrew's characteristic attitude was to take things cheerily as they came, because they were from the hand of God. Sometimes his meetings were in a church, sometimes at a gathering of tents and wagons, sometimes in the open air, even in the moonlight with candles lighted only during the singing. Often he traveled at night in order to reach another group by early morning.

His burning love for the Lord and his intense earnestness for the spiritual welfare of his people brought him much heart-searching. "When I look at my people, my peace forsakes me. . . . I tremble at the thought of my people's personal accountabilities for refusing my messages. . . . I am obliged simply to flee to the Master I serve and to seek for a new and more entire surrender to His work. . . . Oh! that the coming year of my ministry may see me more and more a *minister of the Spirit.*"

Andrew's overwhelming schedule took its toll, and without time to rest between discharging his enormous duties the strong and healthy young man became worn out physically. He wrote to his father, "I trust that I shall be continually accompanied by your prayers; and oh! I care little whether I have strength enough or not, if only my own soul were but in a fitter state for commencing such a solemn work. Oh! for the anointing of the Spirit for my unclean lips, and His softening and enlightening and renewing grace for all who hear!"

7

Vacations for Spiritual Trek

As if his own 50,000 square mile parish were not enough to fully challenge his efforts, Andrew's missionary heart was burdened for the 7,000 emigrant farmers who had wandered still further north beyond the Vaal River, into the area known as Transvaal. Their children lacked education, secular and spiritual, and the farmers had no opportunity for the sacraments of the church or to hear the Word of God.

Andrew was not authorized by his appointment to spend any of his prescribed parish time in such outreach, so although desperately needing his own physical refreshment, he took his six weeks annual holidays to go over the Vaal in strenuous mission trips. To compound the difficulties, it was the rainy season, there were no roads, and sometimes up to fourteen hours in the saddle were required between outposts. Often forty services were conducted among the six scattered stations. When preaching to the nomadic and unsettled farmers, the meetings were held in the open and under tent sails spread from wagon to wagon.

Early on the first tour, he caught what seemed at first to be a chill, later a fever, which continued off and on throughout the trip. The deacon who was accompanying him, and who apparently suffered from the same symptoms as Andrew, died when he reached home. The Delagoa Bay fever was suspected as it had been spreading with alarming rapidity throughout the Transvaal. Andrew lay for many weeks very near death in a tent instead of a hospital, attended by old Dutch ladies who loved and almost worshiped him. He recovered, but the sickness had been very hard on him. He was described by a friend, "instead of a strong, healthy, rosy-faced man six feet tall, he seemed to have shrunk into a bag of mere skin and bones, and looked like a living skeleton."

When he returned to Bloemfontein, a doctor told him, "I am afraid you will never preach again. Be content to spend your life on a sofa." But God had only begun to work His image in Andrew Murray.

Beside the obvious spiritual successes of his ministry in the Transvaal, his trips there had far-reaching importance relating to political issues. The Transvaal settlers were highly suspicious toward ministers of the Dutch Reformed Church because they were appointed by the governor and paid from public funds. These rebellious farmers wanted little to do with anything that smacked of British control or the "establishment," and that included a young minister who answered to a British colonial governor.

But Andrew's earnest zeal and genuine love and care for the welfare of these emigrants knit their hearts to him. They saw that he brought them ministrations of God's grace at the cost of great physical impairment to himself. His influence went so far as to restore some of their confidence in the Cape Dutch Reformed Church and even fostered a desire to remain a part of that ecclesiastical communion.

Andrew made two further vacation visits to the Transvaal and so endeared himself to the people that they begged for him to be assigned to their territory as his parish. They petitioned the church councils over and over to release Andrew for this wilderness pastorate. His heart longed to accept but he was neither allowed to, nor did it appear to be the will of God for his ministry at that time. But because of his great burden for these people, and for the thousands in his own parish, he continued to expend himself, literally galloping from one preaching session to another.

He reflected in a letter, "It sometimes makes me unhappy to think that I must preach God's Holy Word with so little preparation, and though circumstances prevent my studying much, yet I long to live much more in a state of mind which would be a continual preparation. Oh! could I but live more in heaven, breathing the spirit of God's Word, the Lord would abundantly make up the lack of regular study."

Andrew's training in Scotland under the scholarly and spiritual guidance of his uncle gave him an excellent background to grasp the significance of the times and to be in a mentally alert position to mold current events for spiritual ends. This made him a power for good in his own country on many levels, not only in the religious field.

He was genuinely concerned with the welfare of the people in the Orange River Sovereignty when a protest was launched, after much debate and upheaval among the people, against the decision of the British government to abandon the country. Andrew had been an integral part of the official proceedings and involved in the committee matters to the extent that he and Dr. A. J. Frazer, an army surgeon who had settled down in the Sovereignty, were chosen as delegates to go to England to lay before the Ministry an extensively signed petition against abandonment.

Andrew was pulled in both directions: to decline the appointment, but also to go if there was a possibility of doing his country a service. His own health was another reason for considering a leave, because his extreme weakness dragged on. He described it as "a weakness in my back, legs, and arms, with a sort of nervous trembling in my hands." He felt that the long voyage with the benefit of sea air and a change of pace might help to restore him. (He was twenty-five at the time.) After much prayer and consultation with his family he decided to go, and left in January, 1854.

Before they landed in England, events had taken dramatic turns back in South Africa, and articles were signed at a convention in Bloemfontein that guaranteed in the fullest sense the independence of the country, finally freeing them from allegiance to Britain; the Orange River Sovereignty was changed into the Orange Free State, fortunately unaccompanied by bloodshed. Thus the mission of Dr. Frazer and Andrew was a lost cause which they could scarcely make efforts to pursue. As an unfortunate by-product, the political implications of that trip caused considerable suspicion against him in his home country.

While Andrew was in London, people began to take notice of his fame as an earnest and deeply spiritual young preacher and he was invited to fill many preaching engagements, even invited to occupy the pulpit of the noted Surrey Chapel. Knowing that he should not expend himself because of his health, and longing for a rest, he wrote to his sister, "Perhaps I ought not preach at all. But I find it difficult to refuse altogether, since preaching is, in fact, most refreshing to myself."

He spent some time in Holland and Scotland, proposing to find young men who would be willing to go to South Africa as ministers and teachers. He had no good fortune to find such men and his conviction grew clearer and more urgent that South Africa needed to establish a theological seminary of its own.

While he was in Scotland, his health further deteriorated. "I feel my strength so worn that I do not believe that even perfect rest for three or four months would restore me, and a single summer in Africa would lay me prostrate. The doctor says that my whole system has been much more seriously affected than I have any idea of and that prolonged rest is necessary to restoration. He advises that I should not leave before winter. . . . What I chiefly suffer from is the pain in my hands and arms. Half an hour's lively conversation, or earnest application to anything that requires thinking, immediately makes itself felt there. I cannot even write a note without feeling the pain in my arms. . . ." As it turned out, he was absent from South Africa for a year and nine months, and the welcome he received from the people of his parish upon his return was overwhelming.

Covered Wagon Honeymoon

"There will be another guest at the table tonight, my dear," announced Howson Edward Rutherfoord to his wife, who was always as eager as her husband to show hospitality to God's servants.

"Is it a minister?" Mrs. Rutherfoord questioned, as her youngest daughter, Emma, entered the room.

"Indeed, and a young one at that, to whom I've taken quite a fancy. He has just returned from England."

Emma picked up her needlework and became intensely interested in the direction of the conversation. "Is he English, Papa? How old is he? Is he handsome?"

Her parents laughed. "He's one of the noted Murray sons of the Graaff-Reinet parish. About twenty-seven years old, I imagine, handsome, but on the thin side. Perhaps some good Rutherfoord cooking would fatten him up!" Mr. Rutherfoord chuckled.

Apparently the food and the companionship served to draw Andrew to accept repeated invitations to dinner at the suburban Cape Town home of the prominent English family. The whole well-educated household took to him immediately because of his wide cultural interests and they described him as "a good talker but always ready to listen." But it was lovely Emma with whom he would stroll in the garden at twilight — and it was uncertain as to who was listening to whom.

The Rutherfoord family had emigrated to South Africa and soon acquired a position of prominence in business and in the cultural community. Mr. Rutherfoord was further known for his association with the worthy cause of the "Cape of Good Hope Society," established for aiding deserving slaves and slave children to purchase their freedom. Living in a suburban home with ample space, the family was famous for its generous hospitality to missionaries of every society and denomination, although the Rutherfoords continued as members of the Church of England.

It appeared to be love at first sight between Andrew and Emma and a whirlwind courtship followed. Her father was delighted when Andrew asked permission to marry his daughter. In fact, Andrew wanted to marry her immediately, but Emma didn't want to be *that* rushed. The couple corresponded for a year until Emma was twenty-one, after which Andrew returned to pursue the matter; he was determined not to return all the way to his parsonage at Bloemfontein still a bachelor. Presumably he had a way with words to convince Emma of his pitiful loneliness there and his need of someone to nurse him when he was ill, and how difficult it would be to make that long trip again. He won the eager consent of Emma and a quick wedding was planned.

Emma was born and brought up in Cape Town, and was educated at home with visiting governesses and masters to teach her and her sisters the traditional Victorian accomplishments of music, drawing, fancy work, and a smattering of French and German. Her mother taught her routine housekeeping, ordering meals and keeping tradesmen's accounts, but apparently not much actual cooking because it was an age of plentiful domestic help.

Most important, God was preparing a tailor-made helpmeet for Andrew's future literary ministry; it was to a large extent Emma's influence, encouragement, and actual technical help that launched his writing and enabled him to produce so many books. Because of the weakness in his hands from early years, Andrew was prevented from writing very much. Emma was a girl of broad literary background, having been brought up doing an enormous amount of serious reading under the supervision of her mother. Besides, she had the opportunities of listening with intelligent interest to her parents and their friends discussing current events and opinions. She was a bride at twenty-one, mature for her years.

It happened to be a most inconvenient time for a wedding because Emma's father was far from well, her mother anxious about his health, and worried also about her son's departure to England. "And how can we ever get Emma's traditional 'twelve dozen of everything' in the linens department of a bride's trousseau ready in time?"

"Never mind," pleaded Andrew impatiently, "the parsonage is fully stocked—and how can we bring so many things with us by ox wagon anyway?"

It was quickly accomplished, nevertheless, although the hemming of the table cloths and napkins was to be left for Emma to do later.

When Andrew observed the growing quantity of "household necessities" that he would have to arrange transportation for, it gave him amused alarm. But that was nothing to his shock when Emma announced, "Of course I am taking my piano and other specially dear pieces of furniture and china with me!" Andrew may have had visions of fording flooding streams and the two of them floating away on top of a piano, hugging pieces of English chinaware!

But his new bride and family had their way. The expenses of the journey were enormous; it was a bad time of the year to travel in the cold, both for themselves and the transport animals; the wagon had to be the largest obtainable, and the horses alone cost £140. But in the whirl of excitement the young couple did not regret it; it was all part of the fun of their starting a new life together.

Andrew even made a profit on selling the wagon and animals when they reached home, which was a source of pride to the new bride. "I think my husband, though he sometimes frightens others by his bold way of doing things, always knows what he is about."

Emma's mother gave them one of their most valuable wedding "presents" by engaging an English servant, Mrs. Henly, to go under their employ to Bloemfontein. She proved a treasure with all her accomplishments, taking full charge of all operational matters in the new Murray household to relieve her mistress.

The choice of a church for their wedding could have been a sensitive issue as the couple represented two distinct ecclesiastical poles — the Church of England and the Dutch Reformed Church. "Friendly discussions" were necessary but happy compromises made, with the ceremony taking place in the Dutch Reformed Church at Wynberg but conducted in English with Andrew's uncle, a minister of the Lutheran Church, officiating. The date was July 2, 1856, Andrew being twenty-eight.

Their honeymoon of sorts was spent in the covered wagon on their long journey of almost a month to Bloemfontein. Though an arduous trip, the beauty of some of the scenic places they passed through helped to keep stars in the eyes of the young couple. They dined picnic fashion in beautiful lofty mountains, often by rolling streams foaming in beautiful cascades, sometimes traveling until dark or even in the moonlight until 10 o'clock.

Emma first heard her husband preach in Dutch on the Sundays enroute when they stayed over the Sabbath at farm or village settlements. "One thing impressed me very much," wrote Emma to her family. "They often sing a hymn in the *middle* of the sermon to wake the people up! I thought it was time to leave, and prepared to do so, when they all sat down again and continued!" After the two Sunday services on a particular occasion, the couple walked up the mountain "to enjoy its beauty and quiet and read and sing together until sunset, enjoying the grandeur and loneliness of the place."

As they progressed, the journey became very much more difficult, but Emma was thrilled with the experience of camping out at night — "real pioneering" she called it. Snow soon lay quite close on each side as they traveled. "It was so cold," wrote Emma later, "that the only thing to do was to go to bed as soon as possible."

She registered delight at the different customs she observed by traveling inland among the Dutch. "Oh, the multiplicity of children and the size of the babies! Ten or twelve children is the *ordinary* number. I wonder how it is that the Dutch have not swallowed up the land — I never saw such a marrying and children-loving people. If you want to get to their hearts, just admire the babies or talk to the children. My husband is *very* good at both; he understands quieting a baby far better than I do, but then he has even now a little sister of six months and has always had some little brother or sister to play with."

Leaving the mountains behind, they entered the wide, open, monotonous plains of the Karroo, without farms or houses. "When we halt at night, we speedily boil coffee while the animals are unhitched and fed; then out come cakes, bread, butter, milk, and cold meat and these are enjoyed as supper by the fireside in the bright moonlight. We often sing hymns, then have prayers and retire by the light of a carriage lamp. Getting up in the morning is the *most* difficult as my hands get numb with the cold. We were lost a few times; once we lost some goods off the wagon and had to send back three hours to search for it. The man assigned to the task was followed by a wild dog and would have been eaten had not a second man on horseback overtaken him."

The wagon train detoured east so that Andrew might introduce his bride to his family at Graaff-Reinet. Emma was joyously accepted at once and amused at how the younger children adored her husband. Also, she observed, it was from his mother, to whom he was deeply attached, that he got his gaiety and feeling for colors, and scents, and pretty things.

Some insights into the character of Andrew help us understand his very real humanness and make us appreciate still more his deeply serious teachings and writings that rose from actual life experiences. It may surprise us to hear that Andrew was thought by some to be extravagant. His bride defended him against these remarks: "I don't feel anxious. I think it is more that other people are so close and stingy and can so little comprehend large views. If my husband must get a book, he gets a good one. He is fond of giving his sisters presents and they are generally of the best quality."

The last four years of Andrew's ministry at Bloemfontein were to be in a different style: His health would improve, though he would still be far from robust; his duties as rector of Grey College would not be heavy, but they would keep him from wandering too far from his home parish and newly established home. Most significantly, he would have much more time for study and to begin the writing of books which would issue in worldwide influence for God's Kingdom in the years to come.

A significant development in Bloemfontein after his return was the establishment by others of this college for the instruction of youth and the training of men for the teaching profession. Grey College was founded in 1856 and formally opened in 1859, with a Dutch teacher and an English teacher, but no headmaster. Andrew undertook for a time the duties of rector, which included general supervision and the control of the boarding department.

To Andrew, this was a challenge of a different sort. He wrote, "Religious education must, I think, become the watchword of our church before we can expect abiding fruit from our labors. . . ." His brother John must have written him that he hoped Andrew would soon be free of school duties. He replied, "I hardly wish it. I feel deeply interested in the work and do not think it will be too much for me, as long as I have no direct instruction to give. It is an experiment to see what influence can be exerted upon the boys by daily relationships with them. Will the result be more encouraging than preaching? Pray for me that the spirit of faith and love may possess me, that wisdom and diligence may be given me from on high for the work. Our number today is fourteen with the prospect of four more soon."

9

"A New Idea of a Wife"

When the young couple finally arrived at Bloemfontein, instead of the coveted privacy, they were besieged with visitors. In his bachelor days Andrew had kept open house — anyone free to drop in at any time — and the pattern was never really broken.

Apparently they were never alone in the overcrowded house. Andrew's eldest sister stayed with them temporarily, and although not much older than Emma, tried rather tactlessly to show her new sister-in-law how to run her house! Emma had very definite ideas about herself as her husband's *companion* rather than his *housekeeper*, intending to leave Mrs. Henly, her capable maid, to attend to routine matters. But sister-in-law problems were cheerfully compromised and they became the best of friends for life.

Emma took upon herself the monumental task of establishing a healthy, uncluttered, unpressured home atmosphere for her husband so that he could freely work for the Lord. "To make an excitable, earnest spirit like my husband to rest, that is my most difficult duty and my greatest anxiety. A minister seems to be public property and everyone's friend. From six a.m. until nine p.m. we are never sure of not having visitors. People have little sense of propriety: they walk in whether you are at breakfast or dinner, and if at tea time always expect at least a cup of coffee. The consumption of coffee is dreadful! Dutch people are so fond of it. People sit and talk with Andrew for hours. Andrew's opinion must be had about everything and I can well understand how much he needed a wife and companion with the constant drain on him.

"We have so little time to read; all day and night we just start to pick up a book and are interrupted. We have begun reading the *History of the Early Puritans*, *Neander's Church History*, *Brainerd's Life of Prayer*, and *The Earnest Student*. We try to read on certain evenings after we come back from Andrew's meetings or singing nights, but he is often too tired. After reading a quarter of an hour, his throat gets hoarse and then he likes to lie down and have me sing to him.

"Our delightful gardening is a diversion in the fresh air and does rest Andrew besides providing so many delicious vegetables and beautiful flowers and fruit harvests."

"Concerning Andrew's health," Emma wrote home later, "I am sorry to say he is more tired and unwell than I have seen him during our married life. So many services on weekends, with constant company in the home, quite knocks him down; also the standing around with the many details of all that goes on in the parish, with no place in the vestry for him to rest. I am trying to devise all sorts of plans to get a sofa there, for this fatigue will not do. It is strange that he is something like me in that his fatigue always exhibits itself in excitement and restlessness, then it is followed by complete exhaustion. This morning he seems more dead than alive.

"But don't fancy that because of his weakness he is an old shriveled-looking thing! Andrew is remarkably young and fresh looking and exhibits no *outward* signs of weakness; he never knew a day's illness until he overexerted himself in his holy duties. His constitution is good, only overused, and his wife does her best to prevent that now, with the help of God."

Commenting on Andrew's preaching: "His weekday English services are mainly for the young. I am obliged to listen very attentively to all his sermons for he makes me his critic and always expects to know just what I think. I tell him it is good for him that he has a simple congregation for whom he must bring down his ideas to their comprehension. He is obliged to clip his wings or else. I think we would be in some danger if he had a clever and intellectual congregation; he would become too fanciful or too new, if I may use this expression, in his sermons. Now they must be plain and practical, and shorn of the new, varied, and perhaps a little wild interpretations and symbolic meanings that he favors *me* with."

An insight into the close relationship of Andrew and his wife is reflected in her frank recital to her family. "I am anxious to be a good housekeeper. But Andrew *never* finds fault with anything I do and I am afraid I don't understand yet about being economical, though he never says I am extravagant or even hints things might be better. Sometimes I wish he would say so because I know so little. He always listens to my smallest household trouble even with such serious spiritual things on his mind and tries to find me a remedy, and does everything I ask him and gets what I wish. You cannot imagine a more sympathizing, loving husband, so tender and gentle to his little wife.

"Yet he seems made to command, a sort of bishop or little pope among his people. I tell him that I sometimes feel afraid when he is talking to other people, but never for myself. He had so early in life been accustomed to command and act decisively for himself and others that it has imparted a great amount of decision and strength to his character.

"Ah, but you will think I am always praising my husband. I only wish you knew him, I feel sure you would love him. I certainly never knew before that I could be so bound to anyone or love anyone so much. It seems a new faculty I had been perfectly unconscious of before, almost overwhelming in its strength and depth of joy.

"The only tinge of sadness I have, though I would not wish it otherwise, is that his deep earnestness and feeling for the matters of God so often exhaust his physical strength and remind me that he is human and life is uncertain. Yet I know that 'man is immortal till his work is done,' and I pray he may be long spared to be useful in his day and generation."

Emma's prayer was answered in the long life and wide influence for Christ that God honored Andrew with in spite of his lifetime "thorn in the flesh" — physical weakness — which threw him totally on the strength of his Lord.

Emma had no intention of drifting into the traditional pattern of a tame, domestic wife. Andrew's work necessitated his absence for three or four days every two weeks and she was a capable help in looking after all his affairs. She did considerable parish visiting in the village, had a school for colored people* three times a week, a "book evening" when people came to buy hymnbooks, Bibles and other books, handled the accounts for various matters, helped attend to the mountains of his correspondence in the capacity of secretary to her husband, filing his papers and books, being organist of the church, and helping in the Sunday School.

One of their guests was a clergyman from Holland. During the course of conversation with Andrew on sermon preparation, Andrew called to his wife matter-of-factly, "Dear, where did that idea in last Sunday's sermon come from?"

Emma promptly replied, "From chapter five of Brainerd's biography." She was known for always being able to trace the sources of Andrew's ideas to the many books they read together.

"Ha!" said the amazed Hollander, "She must be *the new idea of a wife.*" The traditional Dutch idea was that the wife was just a housekeeper. He added, "Having a living encyclopedia for a wife must be a useful possession!"

Emma had very determined ideas on being a companion-wife and contrasted herself favorably with "other clergymen's and missionaries' wives who are so entirely taken up with household cares as to be quite unable to exert themselves in aiding their husband's labors or in interesting themselves in the parish work, which is totally neglected." She zealously guarded

*In South African terminology, the colored population are those who are of mixed racial descent.

certain quiet hours for reading and talking with her husband. "When Andrew is tired, he is refreshed by a little talk or music or walk with me, without always being in danger of interruption by a servant or child or guest."

But it was not too long thereafter that she wrote to a friend, "Don't be too surprised when I tell you that I intend to present Andrew with another little temptation and interruption to his study in the shape of a little son or daughter next April, if all is well. . . . I cannot yet realize the idea of myself being a mother!" Emma was apparently not the maternal type by nature, and must have realized that her own wings would be clipped when she had a small child to consider. Finding life far too interesting, she did not go into any kind of retirement while waiting for the baby.

After their first child, a daughter, was born, Emma's life did indeed change and she realized what other ministers' wives with children really *did* have to contend with. "A great difficulty with me is not the want of time, but its right management. I cannot write or keep any account of time or study Dutch or count upon *any* peace; baby wakes, people come, duties press, and time flies. . . ." Emma was learning!

If Emma thought herself presumed upon by duties at *that* time, it was nothing to compare with her "extended family" of several dozen boy boarders, ages nine to eighteen, plus twenty "day boys," when the Murrays undertook supervision as rector and wife of the newly established Grey College in Bloemfontein. Added to that, a second child of their own, another girl, was born soon after. Andrew's natural love for young people and desire to influence them spiritually made him a natural for the rector's position. The Murrays moved into the new school buildings not far from the parsonage. They ate their meals with the boys and thoroughly enjoyed conducting prayers morning and evening.

But with all those added responsibilities, Emma did lament, "I am really ashamed to say I get so few chances to read, and what is worse, so little time for digesting books. My poor brain is usually so engrossed with the business and whirl of life that I am almost unfit for intellectual enjoyment!" But because she was so literary minded, she encouraged her husband in that direction to his great benefit — and also to ours of later generations, as readers of his books. Because of Emma's unflagging enthusiasm and drive, Andrew got down to the task of providing suitable reading matter for his people by writing it himself. His brother, John, was already into book writing and publishing.

In fact, Emma may have been a little jealous, for Andrew's sake, of John's success in this line. John's first two books were doing extremely well and she did not see why her husband, whom she considered far more brilliant, should be left behind. "I tell Andrew that his brother is more worthy than he, for he possesses no shining talents or public eloquence to make him so popular, but he is the most diligent in *business*, the most fervent in *spirit*."

She reflected, "I like this bookwriting very much, when we can find time for it, for I am my husband's amanuensis. We are doing another one now in Dutch, after publishing the first one for children." (This was in 1858, when Andrew was thirty years old.) "It is selling well and should pay its own expenses soon. Then in perhaps eighteen months there may be a little profit, enough to invest in doing our next publication. John has been very much blessed in his publications, some of which have been extensively circulated, and have gone through several editions. Cautious, quiet Scotsman that he is, he has always made them pay for themselves. What he loses on one, he is sure to gain on another!"

10

Revival at Last

Barely thirty years old, Andrew had a wide reputation as a young minister of exceptional abilities, earnestness, and intensity of purpose. Invitations to new pulpits were frequent, and repeated, each to larger areas of influence and more cultured people than the pioneers beyond the Orange River among whom he spent his most active years. He continued to refuse, until in 1860 he believed one to be the call of God; it was to Worcester, an important educational center.

This growing township was about a hundred miles east of Cape Town, comparatively accessible, and seemed to need the kind of energetic spiritual guidance for which Andrew was gifted. The emotional ordeal of severing from his pioneer pastorate of eleven years was traumatic, but Andrew had the conviction that God had ordained he should move on.

In retrospect, although Andrew reproached himself continually for not having been as faithful and fruitful in the lives of his people as he had wished, he had given them totally of himself, and the results which flowed from his ministry were in every way remarkable.

Throughout his life and afterward, men and women recounted how it was during the early ministry of "young Mr. Murray" that they were converted or that they more fully consecrated themselves to their Lord through his powerful public preaching and earnest individual exhortations.

His daughter later wrote, "The photographs taken of Father at that young age represent him as a stern-looking man, and my mother often spoke of his hard criticisms of and deep dissatisfaction with himself. He would say: 'My work seems vain, the people have no real consciousness of sin, no real dread of it; there is so much frivolity and lightheartedness as they come so thoughtlessly before God and to His Table, with no real preparation and no heart-searching.' He was constantly probing his own heart and blaming himself for the lack of consecration in his hearers." But God was leading His servant on, and opening out to him, through his own experiences, the secret of a life of victory and peace into which he was to lead many who would never see him. He was being fitted for a world-wide ministry.

Andrew had become as deeply burdened for revival as his father had been — as much for himself as for his people. Outwardly he had intense zeal, and the word "earnestness" occurs over and over in descriptions of him. For this he was admired and praised, and at this very point he was the most introspective and disappointed, because he viewed himself as being so far short of God's power.

"My own work loses much of the value it once possessed even in my own eyes. Somehow I have not yet been able to employ my Lord's strength instead of my own. My prayer for a revival, in which I have become somewhat careless, is held back by the increasing sense of *my* unfitness for the holy work of the Spirit's ministry."

And again he referred to "that awful pride and self-complacency which have hitherto ruled in my heart." It was that experience, and the later insights and victory through it, that gave rise to his famous book *Humility*. It was because Andrew himself had such a battle with pride. "Nothing but a crucified Jesus revealed in the soul can give a humble spirit."

Even as God was searching his heart and pointing out pride, Andrew seemed to have the unconscious inner attitude that it *had to be preaching* that would bring forth revival — that it would depend on what *man* did, even on what *he* did. It is significant that when revival came, it was described as ". . . not as a rule the direct result of the preaching of God's Word" by any particular person, including Andrew! In fact, when the deep work of the Spirit broke out among his people, not only did Andrew not initiate it, or even recognize it, but he opposed it and tried his best to *stop* it. Was it because *he* did not have control of it? In any case, God was in the process of answering his prayers for humility!

God had been breaking up the fallow ground for the outpouring of His Spirit in South Africa for many years. It was all a part of the larger outpouring that was taking place simultaneously in America and Europe. Not only had Rev. Andrew Murray, Sr. devoted every Friday evening to praying for revival, but later other like-burdened ministers united with him in prayer. They prayed consistently for *thirty* years and waited in faith; then the glorious answer came.

Even at Worcester, Andrew's new pastorate, God had raised up a group of revival intercessors, who for many years had worn a footpath to a hilltop overlooking the village so that they might better pray for the people. The minister who preceded Andrew had intensely prayed and worked for revival.

Andrew's induction to this new charge coincided with the first of many significant conferences arranged by the newly opened Theological Seminary of Stellenbosch, to which ministers and elders came from every area. On the agenda were both missions and revival. God was about to do something with His mighty power on both of these issues which the godly men, sincere as they were, thought they somehow could manage.

Concerning personnel for missions, ministers for the pulpits, and Christian teachers, the situation was critical. There were twenty-six ministerial vacancies in the Dutch Reformed Church of South Africa. Andrew gave a moving address: ". . . Where are we to find assistance? Can we devise no plan by which to supply the need? In vain have we written to France, Germany, Switzerland, and America for assistance in carrying out our mission project: no men can be found. . . . How are we to do it unless *we* can find men for the work? . . . It is for these reasons that we think it necessary to commission someone to visit Holland and to bring back a number of ministers and missionaries. . . ."

The resolution was passed with enthusiasm and a committee appointed to launch it. (Typical church organizational procedures!) Passage and expense money had to be raised for the delegate and the enterprise drew widespread attention. Andrew found himself subsequently busy issuing appeals to the churches, visiting congregations, addressing gatherings and stimulating general interest and support. As it turned out, the recruitment was successful in that eleven ministers responded, two designated for the mission field, plus two school principals, two teachers, and four church helpers. However, much human zeal, time and money were expended to still barely scratch the surface of the need.

Looking at it from the vantage point of what God was about to do among His needy people, let it be noted that one of the fruits of the forthcoming revival in the *single* congregation of Worcester was that *"fifty* young men offered themselves for the ministry of the Word, when previously it was almost impossible to find men for the work." God undoubtedly has ways and means by His supernatural power to accomplish all His works, fully supply all needs of personnel and finances, and the power for the tasks, which are beyond our human devisings and zeal — *if* we wait on Him for *His* ways.

What Andrew learned through this experience and his part in the coming revival permeates all of his subsequent teachings and writings in such books as, *The Spirit of Christ, The Key to the Missionary Problem,* and *The Full Blessing of Pentecost.*

How exactly did revival start in South Africa? We will trace the thread of these important events with careful quotes from eye-witness sources. Andrew's induction to the Worcester pastorate took place on Whitsunday (Pentecost) during the previously mentioned conference. Andrew delivered his inaugural sermon from 2 Corinthians 3:8, "How shall not the ministration of the Spirit be rather glorious?" Great numbers of people from outside the congregation attended that worship service in addition to all the key delegates from Dutch Reformed churches throughout South Africa. Great expectations were aroused that the Lord would richly bless the ministry of Andrew in that place. God was preparing, through that united touch upon His people gathered there, not only the Worcester congregation but scattered parishes throughout the country for the remarkable manifestations of the power and vivifying influence of His Holy Spirit coming very soon.

A paper which traced the fresh visitations of the Spirit on His Church in history had been given at the Worcester conference. The speaker then asked, "Is not such a revival equally necessary in South Africa?" He followed by stating the conditions upon which God could be expected to revive His work in the midst of the years. Earnest discussion followed. Another speaker told about the rise and progress of the revival which had recently visited America, and of the circumstances which fostered its growth and spread. These addresses made a deep impression on those attending the conference. Individual members carried back to their homes a new sense of responsibility and of hushed expectation that God *would indeed* lovingly visit His people with fresh outpourings of His grace.

The actual beginnings were very quiet, without any of the special means thought necessary to rekindle the flame of spiritual life. We note that most of the congregations which were represented at the conference were those in which the awakening of religious fervor appeared the soonest. This was seen initially in increased attendance in prayer meetings, with many new prayer circles established. The congregations of Montagu and Worcester were first touched. It was quite amazing that the awakening was not confined to the towns and villages but felt in totally isolated places without outside contacts, even on remote farms, where men and women were suddenly seized with emotions to which they had been utter strangers a few weeks or even a few days before.

As an example, a weekly prayer meeting had been attempted in one of the sections of the Worcester congregation some months before, but so little interest could be whipped up that the attendance remained at three or four. But when God began to move in 1860, young and old, parents and children, without distinction of color, flocked to that prayer meeting, driven by a common impulse to cast themselves before God and utter their cries of repentance. In places where prayer meetings were unknown a year before, now the people complained because meetings ended an hour too soon! Not only weekly but daily prayer meetings were demanded by the people, even three times a day — and even among children.

Still there were those who doubted that this could be a work of God. They had prayed for years for revival but did not recognize God's answer. Strange scenes were witnessed with this rising tide of blessing. Primary sources have not described them in detail, but say that "an outsider, unacquainted with the workings of the Spirit of God, would have called them undiluted fanaticism. . . ." And yet the Lord graciously kept His people from serious excesses.

It is best at this point to quote from an eyewitness, Rev. J. C. deVries, to gain a clearer picture of what happened at Worcester.

On a certain Sunday evening there were gathered in a little hall some sixty young people. I was leader of the meeting, which began with a hymn and a lesson from God's Word, after which I prayed. Three or four others gave out a verse of a hymn and prayed, as was the custom. Then a colored girl of about fifteen years of age, in service with a nearby farmer, rose at the back of the hall and asked if she too might propose a hymn. At first I hesitated, not knowing what the meeting would think, but better thoughts prevailed, and I replied, Yes. She gave out her hymn-verse and prayed in moving tones.

While she was praying, we heard, as it were, a sound in the distance, which came nearer and nearer, until the hall seemed to be shaken; with one or two exceptions, the whole meeting began to pray, the majority in audible voice, but some in whispers. Nevertheless, the noise made by the concourse was deafening.

A feeling which I cannot describe took possession of me. Even now, 43 years after these occurrences, the events of that never-to-be-forgotten night pass before my mind's eye like a soul-stirring panorama. I feel again as I then felt, and I cannot refrain from pushing my chair backwards, and thanking the Lord fervently for His mighty deeds.

While that meeting was going on, it seems that Andrew was preaching in English elsewhere in the church. He was not present during the beginning of the events. When his own service was over, an elder passed the door of the hall, heard the noise, peeped in, and then ran to call Andrew, who returned with him at a run. Our eyewitness continues:

Mr. Murray came forward to the table where I knelt praying, touched me, and made me understand that he wanted me to rise. He then asked me what had happened. I related everything to him. Then he walked down the room for some distance and called out as loudly as he could, "People, silence!" But the praying continued. In the meantime, I kneeled down again. It seemed to me that if the Lord was coming to bless us, I should not be upon my feet but on my knees.

Mr. Murray then called loudly again, "People, I am your minister, sent from God! Silence!" But there was no stopping the noise. No one heard him, but all continued praying and calling on God for mercy and pardon.

Mr. Murray then returned to me and told me to start the hymn-verse commencing "Help de ziel die raadloos shreit" (Aid the soul that helpless cries). I did so. But the emotions were not quieted and the meeting went right on praying. Mr. Murray then prepared to depart, saying, "God is a God of order, and here everything is confusion!" With that he left the hall.

We may wonder at Andrew's attitudes and actions upon that occasion. He had longed and prayed for revival for so many years, and had heard reports in detail on how God was manifesting Himself by His Spirit in other countries, in the same manner as He had on many historical occasions. How was it then that he tried to interrupt, even stop, the work of the Spirit? Although the Dutch church was known for its calm, unemotional approach to religion, it had been *just that* which Andrew deplored, and which, by his own intense zeal and fiery preaching, he had been seeking to break through. Could it have been that his ego was hurt because the moving of the Spirit had not happened as a result of *his own preaching*; in fact, that he had not been present at all to guide it?

It would not do to analyze why Andrew called upon his own authority as their minister sent from God to stop a group in earnest prayer. Moreover, these were young people, who were traditionally respectful and obedient to their elders, especially to their ecclesiastical head. We only conjecture, but from this episode we may nevertheless take our own lessons.

Prayer meetings were held every evening after that. It seems that the pattern was the same each time, although no one set it. At the beginning of the meeting there was generally great silence; no efforts were made to stir up emotions, but after the second or third prayer the whole hall would be moved as before, with no human instigation, and everyone would begin to pray aloud. This was indeed *not* the custom of the Dutch Reformed churches at that time, nor did anyone teach them to do so. Sometimes the gathering would continue until three in the morning; even then, many wished to stay longer. As the people returned to their homes in the middle of the night they went singing joyously through the streets. The number of people participating so increased that the prayer meeting had to be moved to the school building, and that soon overflowed. Hundreds of countryfolk streamed into the village to join in.

On the first Saturday evening in the larger meeting house, Andrew was the leader. Our eyewitness continues:

> Mr. Murray read a portion of Scripture, made a few observations on it, engaged in prayer, and then gave others the opportunity to pray. During the prayer which followed his, we heard again the same sound in the distance. It drew nearer and nearer and on a sudden the whole gathering was praying.
>
> That evening a stranger had been standing at the door from the beginning of the meeting, watching the proceedings. Mr. Murray descended from the platform and again moved up and down among the people, trying to quiet them. The stranger then tiptoed forward from the door, touched the thirty-two year old clergyman gently, and said in English, "I think you are the minister of this congregation. Be careful what you do, for it is the Spirit of God that is at work here. I have just come from America, and this is precisely what I witnessed there."

Andrew apparently needed no further confirmation. It was a crisis time in his own life which catapulted him for the rest of his long life into the deep walk in the Spirit for which he had yearned and prayed.

At this time his father visited him at Worcester and thanked God that he was allowed to be present and speak at such meetings. He said, "Andrew, my son, I have longed for such times as these, which the Lord has let you have."

The same eyewitness tells of a lady who was visiting his parents at the time of these meetings, who later married one of the first missionaries from the area and herself died on the mission field:

> Miss Hessie Bosman was cautioned not to go to the meetings because she was in rather weak health. She replied, "No, I must go, even if it should prove my death; for I have prayed so much for these meetings and longed so much to take part, that I cannot remain away."
>
> She attended, and was the third to engage in prayer that evening. While she was pouring out her heart, the whole meeting broke forth into prayer, and she fell as if unconscious to the ground. I carried her out to the parsonage, where they were some time in bringing her round. But she had not been taken ill, and was none the worse for attending. The next day she was herself again.

Not only did the revival sweep mightily over the congregation at Worcester, but the lives of many individuals were permanently transformed.

11

Fruit that Remains

It is by solid spiritual effects and changes in the lives of individuals and in the community that a true work of God can be evaluated. When the revival in South Africa had passed the stage of vehement emotion and was running a calmer though deeper course, church leaders attempted to catalog its results, which were, in many cases, little less than revolutionary.

In the town of Montagu, a place noted for its indifference to religion, a tone of seriousness about Christian things had permeated the whole community. It was recorded that even those who felt compelled to disapprove of certain features of the revival were obliged to confess that within a few months the general improvement in the conduct of the inhabitants was really wonderful.

In Wellington, which was to be Andrew's later appointment, it was reported to the presbytery that the parish had made greater moral and spiritual progress in the last few weeks than in the course of its history since its establishment. Other communities echoed that record.

It is well known that all revivals have attracted superficial persons, that there is some mass influence of one upon another, and there is counterfeit of the real. But the church leaders were aware of these dangers, and acknowledged that these did not discredit the *genuine* work of the Spirit. They pointed to the great number of persons who were soundly converted at that time — some, open sinners; some, respectable church-goers who, in the sudden light of God's Spirit, realized their own hypocrisy and depravity and repented with overwhelming reality and permanence.

The story was documented of a certain farmer well known for his quiet and retiring disposition, who hardly ever joined in common conversation because of his shyness. Joyously converted during the revival, he was later visited by some of his former friends who had not known of his conversion. They were amazed when this silent man began to witness to them in a bold and deeply earnest and eloquent manner and "with searching look" about the old truths which, through the enlightenment of the Holy Spirit, had suddenly become new to him.

The revival affected all ranks without distinction of age or color. Many youths were touched; those who had been motivated solely by pleasure and were indifferent to the church, after conversion immediately became involved in Christian ministries. Especially were the young people burdened for their still unconverted relatives and friends. Whole households came to Christ through the witness of youths and children.

Nor was the revival limited to the Europeans. Native Africans living upon lonely farms as day laborers, often looked down upon by the rest of the population, were equally touched by the Holy Spirit. A certain native girl in the employment of a farmer's wife was overheard in the fields by the farmer as she wept and implored God to forgive her sins in the name of Jesus Christ. On returning home, he inquired if she had previously shown any interest in her soul. His wife replied, "The girl asked me just yesterday if Christ had died for her as well as white people, and whether she, too, might ask for pardon and peace with God."

Emma wrote to her mother about the meetings: "We are having so many visitors from surrounding places who come to see us on account of the revival. They go away blessed saying that the half had never been told. It is a solemn thing to live in such a congregation at such a time. I feel sure the Lord is going to bless us even more and yet there are heavy trials before us. The work is deeply interesting and yet some things are painful. . . . In the early stage, Andrew came down the aisle and prayed a most solemn, heart-searching prayer that if the work was not of God, He Himself would put a stop to it. The people were terrified as the excitement was very intense. Some even fainted. . . . Andrew is so very discreet in dealing with souls; about twenty came forward last night and others stayed behind to be talked to. We do feel and realize the power and presence of God so mightily. His Spirit is indeed poured out upon us. My little ones are very good so I am able to get out almost every night to the meetings. Andrew is very tired after the meetings but is generally able to sleep well and feels refreshed in the morning."

Not only were the more privileged congregations of the West touched by the Spirit, but the fire spread during 1861 throughout the Central Karroo and beyond, even reviving congregations that were pastorless. It was indeed not a work of man. Yet although no single man instigated the revival, Andrew Murray contributed in a large degree to the diffusion of the blessings of the revival. He had been assured directly by the Lord that he was in the midst of a genuine work of the Spirit, and was himself transformed in a deep inward way.

He began to evidence that power in his ministry that was obviously different from the intense zeal with which he had already so faithfully served the Lord. He had now been taught by the Spirit to let the Lord work *through* him, rather than to generate his own human power even while doing the tasks of God. A man who had heard Andrew preach for the first time wrote, "Much has been told us of the talents of that young preacher, but our tense expectation was far surpassed. We cannot but reiterate the heartfelt conviction that it would be the greatest of blessings for the Dutch Reformed Church of South Africa if she possessed a dozen Andrew Murrays of Graaff-Reinet to give to the church as many and such-like sons as he has given."

At the time Andrew took the Worcester pastorate only one or two of the oldest members had been bold enough to pray aloud in meetings, nor was it permissible for women to take audible part in prayer meetings. The youth were not at all affected in their inner lives or lifestyle by the established church. And no one would be so presumptive as to declare that he was sure that he was converted or regenerated. But with the coming of the revival, it was said, "there was a general movement among the dead bones."

Andrew's preaching took on an intangible supernatural quality that was in very deed "in the ministration of the Spirit and of power." It was as though one of the prophets of old had risen from the dead.

Andrew wrote after the revival: "Oh, if we did not so often hinder Him with our much serving, and *much trying to serve,* how surely and mightily would He accomplish *His own work* of renewing souls into the likeness of Christ Jesus. What secrets He would whisper in the silence of a waiting heart. . . . To my mind, the most striking proof that we truly had the Holy Spirit among us in the late movement is to be seen in what He is *now* doing in stirring up in the hearts of believers a desire after more entire *surrender* to Himself and His service." His book *Absolute Surrender* was seeded in what he observed in this arena of experience.

So many young converts came out of the revival that Andrew was burdened with the need to instruct them how not to lose the blessed intimate relationship with Jesus Christ when they inevitably stepped back into their routine lives and duties. *Abide in Christ* was written to meet this need, and at once became a much-beloved companion for many heaven-bound pilgrims.

Around this period he also published a book for those whose weak faith needed strengthening, titled in English *Why Do You Not Believe?*

12

Urban Parish and
Court Battles

The synod of the Dutch Reformed Church of South
Africa in 1862 honored Andrew by electing him as
moderator, though he was only thirty-four years old.
This was a distinguished mark of confidence in him by
the ministers and elders, because the difficulties of the
synod that year and in the few years following, in the
struggle with the civil courts, were monumental and the
decisions made history.

During this period assaults were made upon both the
doctrine and the constitution of the church. The
rationalistic or "liberal" movement had arisen, which
was all-powerful in Holland. It exercised a subtle but
profound influence over the minds of the young South
African ministers who had received their theological
training in the universities of Holland. "Liberal"
propaganda was everywhere, not only in church
journals but even in public newspapers. The
constitution and government of the church was open to
attack because of its position as an established church
which derived its powers and legal authority from its
connection with the state.

These were difficult years for Andrew officially and personally, causing tension and consuming the energies of a great many of the leaders involved, especially when it went so far as to necessitate lawsuits in court, one even being against Andrew himself. In the course of three years, however, it became evident that the "liberal" movement had spent its force insofar as the South African Dutch Reformed Church was concerned, but not without causing much havoc among the congregations, which in many cases were wounded and split.

That this happened right after the sweeping work of a revival, with its spiritually unifying love, should cause us to reflect on the vicious attempts of Satan to nullify the work of God. But the Enemy was not successful. God's work in the hearts of men continued to flow through His surrendered channels, including Andrew.

One of Andrew Murray's former biographers devotes several chapters to the details of the church and civil controversies at this period. For the purpose of this biography we shall not do likewise, but for the sake of accuracy, and to understand the pressures brought to bear on a spiritually oriented shepherd, we will quote an official summary from the records of the library of the University of Cape Town:

> Trouble started with the suggestion that ministers and elders from beyond the boundaries of the Colony had no right to attend the synod. The synod rejected this proposal and the matter was taken to the civil court where the church lost its suit on the grounds that the Church Ordinance of 1843 was valid only for the

Cape. Immediately the liberal members of the Church took further legal action.

The Rev. J. J. Kotze, of Darling, put forward objections concerning the interpretation of the Heidelberg catechism; the synod rejected his objections and suspended Kotze, who then took the matter to the civil courts. As the barrister representing the synod was ill at the time, Andrew Murray was instructed to conduct the defense of the Church, which he did with a plea lasting four and a half hours.

Regarding the first point, that the presbytery and not the synod constituted the primary court in judging matters of doctrine, the bench was divided. On the second count, irregularity of procedure, and on the third, denial of heterodoxy on Kotze's part, judgment against the Church was unanimous. Immediately after this, charges of dogmatic heterodoxy were brought against a minister, the Rev. T. F. Burgers, later president of the Transvaal Republic, on the grounds that he denied the existence of a personal devil, denied that the person of Christ was without sin, and denied the resurrection of the dead and the continued existence of the soul after death. Burgers was conditionally suspended from office.

When he had recourse to the civil courts, Murray again had to defend the Church. His most important argument was that the Church had spiritual authority, outside the jurisdictions of the court. When the matter was decided against the Church in terms of the Ordinance of

1843, the Church appealed to the Privy Council; and in connection with this appeal, Murray was sent to England. Again the result went against the Church, so that it no longer had the power to suspend ministers who, in its judgment, professed heterodoxy.

During Murray's pastorate at Cape Town, there appeared from the liberal theological side a book by the Rev. D. P. Faure (founder of the Unitarian Church), *De Moderne Theologie*, to which Murray responded with a series of thirteen sermons in 1868. Murray had to defend himself in the public press against accusations that he taught that man was lost or saved through his own free will, that man can frustrate God's will to redeem him, and that God wills the redemption of all.

During Murray's Cape period, several attempts were made, in the face of the threat of liberalism, to effect closer cooperation, if not union, between the Anglican and Dutch Reformed Churches, and Murray served on one of the committees investigating this matter. But in consequence of the Anglicans' view that contact with an institution which denied the episcopacy was impossible, these overtures failed.

In 1864 Andrew was called to fill the vacancy in a joint pastorate in Cape Town. He commented, "If God wills to bless, no instrument is too weak, and blessed it is to be the instrument which He condescends to use." His two fellow-pastors were men of advancing age, and Andrew found himself plunged into a round of many duties which made heavy and ceaseless demands upon his strength.

During his pastorate at Cape Town, Andrew was delegated to go to England in charge of his denomination's appeal to the British Privy Council, as part of his duties as moderator of the synod. This was in 1866. Emma and the children, now five, sailed with him. Shortly after their arrival they received the news of the death of Mr. Murray, Sr., who had retired a few months previously on the grounds of age and growing weakness. He had served the church faithfully for forty-four years. The Murrays were away ten months, during which time a sixth child, a second son, Andrew Haldane, was born.

To show a humorous side to his sternness, an anecdote is told about Andrew preaching in England to two hundred thieves, probably in a prison, on Christmas day. A captive audience, literally, who had not invited him, they began to cough him down when he began to preach. Taking out his watch, he said, "One at a time, gentlemen, one at a time; as the sailor said to the minister while his donkey brayed: 'Either you or the donkey!' So I will give *you* five minutes to cough and you will give *me* five minutes to preach."

At the end of Andrew's five minutes the men were so interested that they forgot to cough any more until the service was ended.

Emma felt very much at home in England visiting her many relatives there. During the European trip, Andrew was invited to many prestigious pulpits and halls of learning to preach, and was offered invitations to more than one very famous pulpit in London. That a man of Andrew's judgment knew what he was doing when he refused the call to stay in London is evident. When Emma asked whether he would accept any of the calls, he replied, "No, my church needs me, my people need me, South Africa needs me. I must sacrifice myself for them." He never spoke of it again as a sacrifice, but threw himself heartily into every sphere of work that the Lord opened before him.

The congregation of Cape Town was an immense one, consisting of more than 3,000 communicant members and some 5,000 adherents. There were two church buildings, one able to seat 3,000 and the other about 1,000. The three ministers preached in the two churches in rotation. It was said of Andrew that he "speedily realized that much more could be done" and that he turned immediately to the less privileged classes who lived in the more remote districts of the city. There were already schools and weekly chapel services but Andrew was challenged to make the activities more productive spiritually.

He was gifted in inspiring others and putting them to work. He wrote an article in the newspaper on the principles of slum work, which he had learned about in Edinburgh. He made the analogy that churches are not like bars, where it is enough to throw open the doors and the longing for drink draws people in. The poor and lost, on the other hand, must be looked up and brought into church. He pointed out that this was not a job for the minister but a labor for Christian laymen, each in charge of certain districts for visitation. "Merely to build schools and churches for the poor is to offer them stones for bread. There must be *living, loving* Christian workers who, like Elisha of old, will take the dead into their arms and prayerfully clasp them close until they come to life again."

He was additionally burdened for the spiritual and intellectual welfare of young men, and in August 1865 became the first president of the Young Men's Christian Association. He was elected over and over and served the Y.M.C.A. productively for many years. Andrew's public, community, and ecclesiastical image grew, but not without some envy and opposition. A satirical piece appeared in print about him, which nevertheless was probably quite an accurate appraisal of his abilities.

One of the men of the ultra-orthodox party, who pose as watchmen on the walls of Zion, is Rev. A. Murray — a worthy leader. Eloquent, quick, and talented, he has an acute mind and clear judgment. He instantly knows the weak points of his opponents' arguments and knows how to assail them. He carries the meeting with him; he is too clever for most. He understands the art of making his ideas so attractive to the elders and the small minds among the ministers (who all look up to him with reverence) that they very seldom venture to contradict Demosthenes, or as another has called him, Apollos. It would be sacrilege to raise a voice against the Right Reverend, the Actuarius, Andrew Murray. There is no member of the Assembly who possesses more influence than he, and certainly no one among the conservatives who better deserve his influence. He is consistent, and consistency always demands respect.

As to his pulpit manner, Andrew was very vehement, and his congregation observed that "bookboard and Bible were soundly belabored." But his personal teaching manner with his catechumens was equally powerful. One of his pupils, later a minister, Rev. C. Rabie, tells us how it was:

"I was one of those privileged to be confirmed by Mr. Murray. He always turned us to the Bible and made us read and explain all the answers. Every time the class was over, he asked two or three to remain and he had a personal talk with them about the condition of their souls. Many of us date our spiritual birth from those talks."

Apparently his pastoral visitation was not tea-and-cakes and chatting-about-the-weather, but "carried terror to the hearts of his parishioners," Mr. Rabie went on. "If his preaching was like thunderbolts from the summit of Sinai, what would personal rebuke be like? Under his individual dealings with them, people felt that they were being ground to powder — in a loving way. On one occasion, at the close of a prayer meeting, Mr. Murray proceeded to deal with each individual present. One lady, observing how her pastor drew nearer and nearer to where she sat, became gradually more and more uneasy, until, as Mr. Murray turned to her, she fell upon her knees crying, 'O Lord, into Thy hands I commend my spirit!' "

Mr. Rabie added that there was a great contrast between the stern young Mr. Murray of those days, and the loving and gentle Mr. Murray whom they knew in later years. God was dealing with His servant differently during each period of his life and Andrew in turn dealt differently with his people as his own experiences matured and mellowed him.

About this stern period, one of his daughters sought to give us a more balanced view of his temperament. She recalled winter evenings when her father would read to the children and dramatize for the younger ones the roars of the lions in missionary adventure stories, "which would cause us great but laughing terror." He took wild romps with his youngsters in the open fields, and on summer afternoons the parents would take the children for a picnic in the hills to engage in games, such as throwing stones at a bottle. They recalled the excitement and joy of the very human and emotional reunions they had when their father returned from long journeys.

During his Cape Town pastorate, Andrew began to devote himself more continuously to literary work. *Be Merciful Unto Me,* a series of devotional studies appearing first in magazine form and then in a book for seekers, was a study in the Fifty-first Psalm. A series of papers followed, titled *God's Word and Error,* but was not finished into a book. He also edited a Christian magazine for several years, one in which some of his own writings had heretofore been published.

The church work in Cape Town did not prosper up to Andrew's expectations due to the system of three pastors, and in 1871 he received a call to a pastorate at Wellington, forty-five miles distant. While considering whether to go, his brother John wrote him, bringing out several considerations that might influence him to stay at Cape Town.

Andrew wrote him back, "That just goes to show how each of us must, in the final, decide for himself. The very things which you think would *influence me to stay* do not weigh with me at all. I don't mind the difficult situation of the Wellington congregation; nor to have all kinds of people, old and young, under my continuous personal influence. Systematic preaching and care of one congregation are to my *liking*. Neither charge throws much into the scale of a possibly better place for a more prolonged life. To possess fixed property here somehow doesn't appear to weigh with me. If it be God's will that I go, He will provide in this matter.

"The argument of someone else that I am indispensable here as representing the church does not appear to reach me. My first work, my calling, is to be a pastor; where I can be happy in this work, thither I feel myself drawn. I do think that I have honestly and in childlike simplicity said to the Father that if He would have me stay here, I am ready and willing. . . ."

It was thus that Andrew waited upon the Lord for every decision. He was quietly confident: ". . . I dare not think that God will leave me to my own devices."

13

Wellington — Pastorate in a Pasture

Andrew did accept the Wellington pastorate in 1871.
Many people in the Cape Town church had felt sure that
Andrew would not leave because at age forty-three he
was "on his way up" and would soon become senior
minister with ever greater prestige and influence. Some
looked upon his decision as a backward step on the road
to fame. Why should he choose the small congregation
at Wellington with its limitations and leave the glitter
of the city and its opportunities for advancement?

But God's ways are not our ways, nor His thoughts
our thoughts. It was that very quiet, contemplative,
country life in Wellington that led to a deeper, truer
knowledge of God and ultimately to the writing of the
many Christian books by which he was made a blessing
to God's people in all lands. God chose for His servant a
less active and less prominent public role; by "pruning"
him and cutting back his labors, God enabled Andrew to
bear much fruit. Surely Andrew reflected on these ways
of God as he wrote the book *The True Vine*, with its
deep spiritual implications.

"Why call Mr. Murray to our church?" an old farmer of the Wellington congregation was heard to remark. "In two years time we will have the expenses of another funeral."

Strenuous labor in past charges and the strife of the synod with the civil courts had left their physical marks on Andrew, and he may have looked to some to be too frail to last very long. But his spirit was robust and exercised, ever deepening his own soul's journey and broadening his influence among men.

The satisfaction of preaching to his own special group of people year after year also proved most beneficial in spite of the hard work to which he committed himself. Andrew was in his prime, and in God's providence was to spend the remaining forty-five years of his life at Wellington, thirty-four of them as pastor.

In contrast to the urban setting of Cape Town, Wellington was described by a visitor as "beauty in the lap of grandeur." A panorama of mountain ranges with rugged peaks, bathed in the setting sun with exquisite rose and purple tints, awed even those who dwelt there from childhood. The lush valleys were lined with vineyards; orchards climbed the hill slopes with their lavish foliage, blossoms, and fruit. The ground was very fertile and the farms were comparatively small, yielding well.

The village itself sheltered only about 4,000 inhabitants, white and colored, but it was the center of a larger and prosperous farming community. Andrew's congregation was also a contrast from his previous charges. Composed largely of descendants of the Huguenots who had fled from persecution in France, they were, in some sense, refugees. French names were as common as Dutch. A deeply religious people, they faithfully attended the services. Especially since the recent revival, many were zealous for spiritual matters.

Wherever the Murrays served, their parsonage became a center of hospitality. Wellington was no exception. Ever since the mountain pass between Worcester and Wellington was opened, communication was easy and the distance not formidable. It also lay on the main road connecting Cape Town with all northern settlements. With a roomy parsonage, streams of visitors were common.

Andrew was immediately plunged into many congregational problems and activities — the liquidation of the church debt, higher education and the training of teachers, local mission work, and church government matters. But he loved his people, making no distinction between the poorest and most ignorant and the rich and wise. Generally they were simple folk, not highly trained academically, but full of practical knowledge of their work and good sense. As Jesus had done, Andrew drew upon the daily lives of his people to illustrate spiritual truths in his preaching, teaching, and most surely in his writing.

His book *The True Vine* was first preached, then written, with the foremost occupation of his people in mind. We can visualize Andrew visiting his parishioners and being taken into their vineyards, asking questions on the nature of the vine growth, and the husbandman's duties, and praying and meditating to receive lessons from God.

But it was this very occupation that some thought would cause an open controversy. It happened that his congregation had not been acquainted with the temperance principles which Andrew had held staunchly throughout his ministry. Soon after he arrived, he started a crusade to close down some of the many public taverns.

"Mr. Murray, you are going to split the congregation apart!" warned an angry wine farmer.

"Never," Andrew replied. "We will, if necessary, take the scissors of *love* and cut it in two, having one side for temperance and the other not, but we *will* live together in *love*." He approached them tactfully, again using illustrations with which they were familiar.

"When a farmer trains a young horse, it will often shy at a stone or something else. The wise farmer will quietly lead the horse to the unfamiliar object and let him look at it and smell it till all fear passes and it will not shy any more. So I will not force temperance upon you. But we will speak and preach about it until you are familiar with it and approve of it!"

And he was successful — the number of saloons dwindled to only four in Wellington, whereas there were, at the same period, forty in the next village.

But his crusade was not without militant opposition. Many people were angry with him and someone tried to burn the parsonage down by throwing lighted kerosene-soaked rags into their windows near the lace curtains. God overshadowed them with His protection.

Andrew was genuinely interested and involved in the advancement of all community causes, whether they were related to religion or not. Through the years, many of his opponents became his warm friends. Even when men opposed him, he still maintained sympathy and communication with them.

He initiated in his new location some of the successful projects that he had founded in Cape Town, among them the training of the members of his congregation to do mission work in the different wards of his parish. He was also burdened for the large number of colored people — day laborers, farm servants, household workers, herdsmen and the like — who were still unreached for Christ by on-going gospel work. To provide for the spiritual benefit of this neglected group, Andrew started Sunday Schools and evening schools for the old and young, with good attendance both in the church mission hall and in the out-districts of the congregation, until they spread to nearly every ward. His conviction was that their own farm people could never be reached properly for Christ unless the masters were also helpers to instruct the servants about the gospel. The colored people showed great eagerness for these opportunities.

Although concentrating on one congregation, Andrew was in great demand as an evangelist, and accepted invitations to conduct other meetings as he was able. He trained his own congregation as a "back-up team" to help in his work by prayer. Many of his writings, such as *The Ministry of Intercession* and *The Prayer Life*, had their foundation in these instructions. He wrote back to his people from a meeting, "I feel anxious to get God's people together to point out the need of intercession and entire consecration.... I have a strong feeling that God will give our people the spirit of prayer to ask and expect new and more mighty blessings when I return. . . . I beseech you to pray for a more powerful work of the Holy Spirit.... Stir up the people to pray for us."

Andrew was quick to enlist prayer partners for God's Kingdom, believing that prayer was the only channel to secure the workings of God in the lives of men. When a number of retired farmers came to live in the village, Andrew suggested that God had brought them there to become intercessors, and set about to train them for that work. He was an example to the believers by his own consecration. His famous prayer for himself was:

"May not a single moment of my life be spent outside the light, love, and joy of God's presence. And not a moment without the entire surrender of myself as a vessel for Him to fill full of His Spirit and His love."

Andrew endeavored never to preach what he did not practice, especially in the area of prayer. Andrew's habit was to enter into a small book the lists of subjects for which he was making special prayer requests. Opposite each were recorded the answers from God. A recurring request was, "For the power of the Spirit in all my work, *that it be not done in my own strength.*" Another was, "That I may endeavor in preaching to make clear this truth of main importance: that conversion is surrender of sin — of *all* sin." And in the middle of a building program of the seminary, "Let me feel that when once I have *cast* my cares upon Thee, they are Thy concerns and not mine, and that Thou wilt do all for me. May I have grace with *stones* and *bricks* and *wood*, with all the burdens, and workmen, to trust and pray and rest in Thy faithfulness who never fails."

An intimate prayer was jotted down on a back page, "Infinite God: Make me empty and fill me full of Thy Holy Spirit and love, full to overflowing, that then this weary world may see and drink. Full of Thy love to me: full of love to Thee: full of love to them: full, myself, of love, of lovingkindness to everyone."

The golden ray of prayer illumined all Andrew did. Like Luther, he believed that nothing that was amiss and demanded correction could not be corrected or endured by prayer. The striving of his human spirit to attain, particularly through prayer, to the blessedness of daily and uninterrupted communion with God may be regarded as the secret of Andrew's spiritual strength.

Andrew was aware that some have contended for each of the sides of the question: Does prayer change things (the objective influence of God) or is the main value of prayer that it changes the people *that pray* (the reflex influence upon us)? Andrew took the position that although the exercise of prayer can either calm us into peace or raise us into ecstacy in the presence of the Father, yet this is *not* the teaching of our Saviour. "If we carefully study all that our Lord spoke of prayer, we shall see that everywhere He urges and encourages us to *offer definite petitions* and *expect definite answers.*"

In 1883 Andrew founded the Bible and Prayer Union, the main object of which was to encourage members of his church to read the Scriptures daily and to pray regularly for specific causes. To this end each member annually received a calendar with daily lessons and a prayer list, as well as some useful book, for a mere shilling a year. The Union started on a modest scale, but its membership increased to 20,000. Expenses were met, and it brought spiritual support and blessing to thousands throughout the country. For more than forty years Andrew was the editor of its daily devotional, *Uit de Beek* (Out of the Spring).

There was a very deep work of grace in many hearts at Wellington so that a large proportion of the congregation was truly seeking to live for God. Many of their most sacred experiences centered around the remarkable communion services held in the church. A Murray daughter later described them: "Can one ever forget the times when 500 or 600 communicants would gather around the Lord's Table, and the holy influence of the Lord that permeated the church! Can we forget the holy awe, the deep reverence, the joy and often the rapture written on Father's face when 'Heaven came down our souls to meet'? I remember once that Father seemed to have really been taken up to the third heaven and such a deep solemnity rested on us all before he spoke again with the words, 'I live, yet not I, but Christ liveth in me, and that life which I now live in the flesh, I live in *faith,* the *faith* which is in the Son of God *who loved me* and gave himself for me.' More especially Father emphasized those words '*who loved me.'* Oh the wonder of it that we so little understand! Let us love Him and trust Him more and more!

"We left the Table feeling that we had indeed been fed on heavenly manna, and rose with a deeper love and fuller determination to do and dare all for our adorable Lord and Master. We were strengthened and refreshed as with new wine, and in the Thanksgiving Service afterward there was a time of wondrous praise, not from the lips alone, but from the heart. . . ."

Andrew's holy and important estimation of the sacrament of The Lord's Table is set forth in a deeply beautiful and Biblical way in his book by that title. He imparted the same value of it to his people, and was most grieved when congregations took lightly their participation in this service.

During this early period at Wellington, the Murray family both decreased and increased, by joys and sorrows. Because there were few suitable high schools for girls in South Africa, the Murrays decided to send their two eldest daughters, Emmie and Mary, ages 14 and 13, to the Moravian Institution at Zeist in Holland for two years. Their father carried on a detailed correspondence to encourage and instruct them, doubtless remembering his own need for such when his brother John and he left the family circle so young to study in Scotland. He wrote to them tenderly on their level, recounting things they would be interested in, and instructing them about common matters. A few excerpts will show his love and care:

"Dearest child, we have been asking the Lord this morning, should you perhaps feel somewhat sad and desolate on your birthday today, that you will be led to feel that Jesus is near. Do try to get and keep hold of the precious truth that there is *no friend like Jesus* and that even when we feel naughty and foolish or sinful He still loves us and wants us to come to Him with all our troubles, that He may heal and comfort us. . . .

"I hope that the difficulties that trouble you will gradually smooth down. But remember, when difficulties won't accommodate themselves to your wishes, there is nothing like you accommodating yourself to them! This is part of true wisdom and in time takes away the unpleasantness. . . . Don't forget, the object of school life is not so much to impart a large amount of information, but to cultivate those powers by which you can, afterwards, gain information for yourself. And for the calling out of these powers and the cultivation of the habit of application and careful thinking, those studies are useful in which the feeling of interest and pleasure appears to be sacrificed to a sense of duty.

"When traveling up a hill last week, one of my companions was criticizing a road, and pointing out how much better it might have been made. When we got a little farther up the hill, we saw that he was wrong. People at the foot of a hill cannot understand the reason for all the windings of the road, but as they rise higher they discover them. You are just now only beginning to climb: follow in trust the path by which you are led. Afterwards you will understand better than you do now . . . .

"You seem to have some difficulties to see true children of God, your classmates, indulging in conversation or other activities which appear to you wrong. Ask Jesus to help *you* to act up to the light of *your* conscience. If their conscience is not fully enlightened on a point, that may be an excuse for *them*, but cannot be for *you*.

"Try and think, my dear little girls, that you are not too small to exercise influence. Your Uncle John and I thought so too when young, but we found we did exercise some considerable influence in matters among our young friends. Don't argue with others and don't condemn them, but simply try to show that there is a way of being engaged in religious exercises all day without being sad or unhappy, and invite them to join you in such things as reading and singing.

"I ordered for you immediately some good books for your Sabbath reading, and to loan to your friends. . . .

"The weather is beautiful now that spring has come, and Papa has begun his gardening. It has been perfectly exquisite to be out of doors. I think how pleased I shall be when my girls come back and I can show them what a nice garden I have succeeded in making.

"Love the Lord Jesus very much, and do love each other fervently and be very gentle toward each other as the Bible says."

One of the Murray daughters of only eight months died just before their departure for England in 1866. And again while their two daughters were abroad, two more little ones, Fanny and Willie, died in the same year with illness. Andrew had to console his absent children in Holland, as well as himself, his wife and the other children. In beautiful trust and acceptance of God's perfect plan, they all confirmed their own surrender to the Lord again.

In November of the following year, a new son was born to the Murrays and Andrew shared the joyous news by correspondence with his absent daughters.

Whenever Andrew passed through some special experience, joyful, difficult, sad or perplexing, he was always attentive to what the Lord was teaching him. He felt that it was generally a call to some special writing, or to some new service for the Lord. The death of his little daughters and son became to him a fresh call to teach his people to evangelize and train their children, and the children and youth of his country. A great work of Christian education was launched by this new vision of Andrew's.

14

Commit to Faithful Persons

The most important ministry which Andrew undertook in the early days of his Wellington pastorate had to do with the chronic question of supplying the need for more laborers for the Lord's harvest. He received the perception from God that the normal, logical, and most available on-going source was *from the Christian homes of his own country* — rather than continually depending on resources of personnel from abroad.

Although avidly recruiting what we may term "full-time Christian workers," Andrew had a definite philosophy about every believer's responsibility before God. "Every Christian is called to be a worker for God. The secret of a truly religious education is to train our sons with *this* as the great thought of their lives — that they not only belong to the Lord, but each one must work for Him. Work for Him must be the *main object*, not a *side issue*. In whatever position or business they are, they must know that they live only to serve the Lord, and to say of *all* their money, their influence, their talents, 'I hold my life every hour at Thy command!' "

In the denominational magazine he wrote a series of articles which were widely circulated and influential. He made an irresistible appeal to all Christian parents in the land to consecrate their children to God's service and in this way to be willing to let the Lord call them to the home and foreign field, in Christian service as well as to other occupations.

He answered every objection that the parents might have. He pointed out that the Lord has a right to our children; the Lord needs our children, and will Himself indicate to the believers which children He would have and could use. He answered the excuse of parents that they had no money to educate their children; and the excuse that their children may not have the necessary abilities; and the excuse of having an only child; and that some had only daughters.

On this latter point, God gave Andrew new insights which were ahead of his times, and greatly forward-looking in what might perhaps be considered a backward land. "Is there no place in the special service of God for our daughters?" He maintained that there most certainly *was*, but even if there wasn't, he declared, "the consecration of your daughters to God can never be a vain and idle matter. The Lord has latterly shown that He can use women to perform great and important services for His Church; and if parents only will present their daughters to the Lord, He will know how to prepare a sphere of work for them — as intercessors for others, as laborers in His Kingdom, in nursing the sick, or in caring for the poor. Parents who train their daughters with this in view, in faith and prayer, will assuredly experience that their labor is not vain in the Lord."

Then Andrew singled out a special capacity in which women can work for the Lord — that of teaching and general education, carried out by Christians of firm conviction. There were many teachers, he pointed out, who just teach to earn their living and don't really care for the spiritual lives of the children. "May the day soon dawn when many of the young women of our church, with training, will devote themselves to feeding the lambs solely at the impulse of the love of Jesus." This was a banner plea for Christian education which Andrew did not feel should be left in the wishful-thinking stage.

"What are you reading that engrosses you so, Andrew?" asked Emma one day during Christmas vacation. "I can hardly rouse you for mealtime."

"Oh Emma, the example of this book urges me to a mountain task — I can hardly wait to start climbing!" Knowing how to incite Emma's curiosity, he added, "Moreover, it is about a woman."

Emma picked up the book from Andrew's lap and read, *"The Life History and Work of Mary Lyon.* And who is she?"

"The founder of the Ladies' Seminary* at Mount Holyoke in Massachusetts in the United States. One day we must go to America and see that institution for ourselves. It is just the kind of thing that South Africa needs. By God's enabling, *we shall have it!"*

With Emma's eager and faithful writing help, another series of articles was born from Andrew's heart, published in the church magazine at intervals during 1873.

Andrew could not wait for the dragging feet of others to initiate such an important task but was already

*Known today as Mt. Holyoke College.

at work on a practical plan to erect at Wellington a similar institution which would be openly Christian, with an entirely Christian faculty, and domestic arrangements to be performed by the pupils themselves. The fees were to be low enough that even the lower income families might be able to send their children.

On June 25, 1873, the Huguenot Seminary to train young girls for educational work was established. The members of his congregation responded heartily to their pastor's project. Funds were raised from many places, including Andrew's travels for that purpose. The formal opening took place in January, 1874.

From all parts of the country young ladies began to arrive, both to teach and to learn. When classes opened, the building was already too small and a wing was added immediately. Still exploding enrollment necessitated another new building. Two thousand people attended that ceremony and congratulatory letters and telegrams poured in from a distance. So successful was the undertaking that it attracted widespread attention; even visitors from other countries came to see it.

Several teachers from America, from Holland, and England gave the faculty a good academic standing, and the standards of the curriculum were high, comparing favorably to the best institutions for training teachers. Andrew had adopted Mary Lyon's maxim with zest, and it took hold everywhere: "First the Kingdom of God, but after that, most certainly, all science and knowledge."

Andrew had been bold to ask for a teacher directly from Mount Holyoke to be sent to South Africa, guaranteeing her salary; they sent two, who were the excellent pioneers of the whole project. To crown the success of the first year, many of the girls who were not Christians when they enrolled had definitely been won to Christ.

In visiting down-country congregations, Andrew was shocked to see "how much ground we have already lost with the young people by the influence of worldly teachers, and we have not an hour to lose if we want by means of pious teachers to win the younger generations for the Lord. Oh, what a tragedy that Christ's lambs are given to the charge of the world!"

Andrew engaged in many "collecting tours" during the years of the establishment of the Huguenot Seminary. Andrew's philosophy on the raising of money may be summed up in his words: "My brothers, if this is God's work, He surely has enough money to dispense. When He has opened heart and mouth and eye, He will not leave the hands closed. When a matter is made plain to our congregations, they give willingly. . . . It is God's part to care for the money, and ours to discover what the will of the Lord is, and what work we ought to perform for Him — and then in faith to begin it."

But Andrew's travels were multi-purpose, which he sums up in a letter home: "The collections were fair, the interest in consecrating children to the service of the Lord fair, the meetings not without fruit, the preaching not unblessed." But Andrew's call from God was far from giving fund-raising a very high priority. He was a pastor and an evangelist. This set off a struggle in his own heart.

He wrote his wife: "The more I travel, the more I see that the *great* need of our church is *evangelists.* And though I cannot in the least see it would be possible for me to give up Wellington, or to arrange for long absences, it does almost appear wrong not to undertake the work of evangelism when one knows that there are hundreds ready to be brought in. It appears terrible to let them go on in darkness and indecision when they are willing to be helped.

"I have been much struck in reading the notes on Exodus by the words of God to Pharaoh: 'Let my people go that they may serve me.' God does hear the cry and sighing of the thousands of seeking ones and wants His servants to lead them out of bondage. And how can I help saying that if He will use me, I shall only consider the honor too high.

"It makes me sad to preach one or two earnest evangelistic sermons, to see the impression made, and to go away feeling sure that if I could devote a little more time and individual attention to the work, many souls would come to light and joy."

That gave Andrew increasing discomfort about spending even as much time as he did on fund-raising. "The thought suggests itself whether with such precious opportunities, so short and rare, it is right to preach a sermon in order to get a collection, no matter how worthy the project. May the Lord direct and guide. We have said and do say that *entire* consecration to His work and will is our choice and our life. And we know that for all difficulties and questions that come, we have an infallible solution in the assurance that Christ who lives our life in us, *is* sufficient for all that comes and will guide and keep us in perfect peace."

There were times when he apparently did not meet the high quota of funds which he expected, and the question was raised whether that particular journey had been the Lord's will or not. Andrew gave us an excellent insight into his views on success and failure when looking at anything from God's vantage point.

"You think because I have not been so successful that this is a sign that the journey is not the Lord's will? I think we must be careful in judging thus. Either failures or successes are sometimes our most dangerous temptations sent to test our principle. We cannot judge our path by this, for God may have sent it to try us.

"The great thing is to have our minds always in a childlike state when we are considering or fixing our plans — and thus we shall know that God is guiding our path, even if it were a mistaken one, to very blessed issues. Failure, though perhaps I ought not even call it failure, even though I have not got quite as much collection as last time — but even comparative failure, has not for one moment made me think I was not in the right path.

"But one thing has been very heavy on me all through — the idea of being on a mission for *money*, and having no time or opportunity to work for souls. . . ."

Finally he rested in his own recommitment: "I have this day sought to lay myself afresh on the altar and to look to the Great High Priest presenting me to the Father, an acceptable and accepted sacrifice, and engaging by His Holy Spirit to appropriate and use the sacrifice. The need and want of dealing with souls rests heavy upon me. But whether there is any prospect of *my* doing the work, I cannot say. Or whether by training *others* — workers, teachers and missionaries — the Lord may permit me to do *more*, I don't know. But it is just so sad to see souls by multitudes seeking and not finding, sighing and not helped, apparently because there is none to show them the way of the Lord!"

Andrew ultimately realized that by providing the Christian training opportunities for those who would be pastors, teachers and evangelists in the future, he was *reproducing himself* and his own vision and zeal — and accomplishing more for God's Kingdom than if he decided to drop everything and do evangelistic work alone.

God gave His servant Andrew ample days to accomplish each of the different callings on his life and ministry which God had ordained. His longing to devote himself fully as an evangelist was certainly satisfied and crowned with tremendous spiritual success at an age when most men feel the work of their lives is finished. In his very advanced years he was led to break through the conventions of a lifetime and get into personal touch with seeking souls of any age group and gather a whitened harvest for his Lord. Because Andrew was able to spiritually discern God's will and priorities for his ministry at each point in his life, he did not haphazardly abandon a clear call from the Lord to jump into another, no matter with what intense urgency it was laid before him. "Waiting upon God" was truly the hallmark of his life, expressed richly in his book by that title.

Andrew was influenced at this time by the revivals and evangelistic movements in other lands, and asked the Lord how the lessons learned from these movements and men of God might be adapted to the South African situation. He received via Edinburgh an account of the work of D. L. Moody in America, with reports of his addresses and statements of his methods. He prayed over and discussed these things with other pastors and co-workers, particularly the possibility of beginning "after-meetings" of a type which D. L. Moody employed.

Again, waiting on God was his watchword. He held back in launching these until God had given them all clear assurance that this should be done. And it was not until after ten days of prayer meetings with his own church, pleading with the Lord for a moving among the unsaved, that he began to hold such after-meetings. The Lord blessed immeasurably in the next five weeks of evangelistic meetings and workers were in the church until late at night dealing with anxious inquirers.

15

"Quite a Lion" in America

Andrew's first trip to America was in 1877 in connection with his re-election as moderator of the synod, and his representation of the Dutch Reformed Church at the Pan-Presbyterian Council meeting in Edinburgh, Scotland. His younger brother Charles, who had succeeded their father as minister of the church in Graaff-Reinet, accompanied him and the other appointee, Rev. Colin Fraser. For Charles it was a breathtaking first trip to both continents and he kept a journal of their whirlwind schedule, much impressed by the important people in Christian and educational fields whom they were meeting everywhere, and the famous pulpits and meetings where his brother was invited.

"On Andrew's back," he wrote home, "not literally, but metaphorically, *I* get in anywhere! In the circles in which we move, Andrew is quite a lion . . . !"

After the council was finished, Andrew had several additional goals for his tour: to see the condition of the Church and education, and the state of the spiritual life in each country. He looked forward with the greatest pleasure to meeting some of the men whom God had raised up as "witnesses of what He can do for His children." He hoped to see the work of Moody and Sankey since "gray-headed ministers in England and Scotland have acknowledged how much they have learned from these men. And there are other evangelists who have not exactly received a ministerial training but whose enthusiasm and gifts have in many instances been highly instructive to those who are engaged in the regular ministry of the Word."

He wanted to observe what was being done in another area for which he had been burdened in his personal ministry. "What endeavors are there to lead those who are already within the fold to *a deeper comprehension of Christian truth and privilege?* If there is one thing which the Church needs, it is labor directed to this end. The more we study the state of the Church of Christ on earth, the more is conviction strengthened that it does not answer to its holy calling. Hence the powerlessness of the Church against unbelief and semi-belief and superstition, against worldliness and sin and heathenism. The power of faith, the power of prayer, the power of the Holy Spirit, are all too greatly lacking. God's children, in the first place, require a revival — a new revelation by the Holy Spirit of what is the hope of their calling, of what God does indeed expect from them, and of the life of power and consecration, of joy and fruitfulness, which God has prepared for them in Christ. . . ."

Actually, the chief object of his visit to America was to find teachers — and above all, lady teachers — for the Huguenot Seminary and its daughter institutions. When he returned to South Africa months later, he brought with him fourteen lady teachers, twelve from America, one from Scotland, and one from Holland, as well as the minister brother of one of the pioneer teachers from Mount Holyoke with his wife and five children. A successful recruiting, indeed!

They saw most of the things which Andrew had hoped to see, besides getting acquainted with the Dutch Reformed Church in America, and making an eagerly anticipated visit to Mount Holyoke Seminary. The invitations to speak were so many that Andrew and Charles had to separate to accept more of them. Charles, understandably in the shadow of Andrew, but evidently strong in his affection and respect for his older brother, addressed himself to the students at Amherst College, "You must please understand that I am not *the* Mr. Murray; I am *the other* Mr. Murray!"

As to the just-concluded Pan-Presbyterian Council in Scotland, Andrew sent back many reports to the church magazine. He was much impressed with the presentation of missions by his esteemed friend Dr. A. Duff, of India, to whom he referred as "the prince of modern missionaries."

Andrew reported, "Speaking as one of the prophets of old, Dr. Duff said that he wished to bear witness to one matter especially, namely, that missions are not *one* of the activities of the Church, but the *only* object for which it exists. 'I wish,' said Dr. Duff, 'to take the highest possible Scriptural ground with reference to the sole and supreme duty of the Church of Christ to devote all its strength to this cause. With the exception of the brief apostolic age, there has been no period in the history of the Church when this has been actually done — to the great shame of the Church and the unspeakable loss of this poor world. Holding this conviction — a conviction that has been gathering strength during these past forty years of my life — you will not take it amiss in me, standing as I do upon the verge of the eternal world, when I give expression to my immovable assurance that unless and until this supreme duty is more deeply felt, more powerfully realized, and more implicitly obeyed, not only by individual believers but by the Church at large, we are only playing at missions, deceiving our own selves, slighting the command of our blessed King, and expending in all manner of fruitless struggle the powers, the means, and the abilities which should be devoted with undivided enthusiasm to the spiritual subjugation of the nations. . . .' "

Andrew commented earnestly, "All that I have heard, both in America and in Scotland, concerning the missionary enterprise, has wrought in me a deeper conviction that our church has been planted by God in South Africa with the purpose of bringing the gospel to the *native peoples* of the continent of Africa; and that, if this work is to be done, we must have an institution where our sons and daughters can be trained to fulfill it . . . ."

With his keen spiritual perception, Andrew made one reference to an unfavorable aspect of the council meetings. "The same observation has frequently been made of our own synodical meetings. When a large number of God's servants meet in order to consult about the interests of His Kingdom, and about the work they have to perform in connection with it, one would expect that their first felt need would be to place themselves as servants in the presence of their Lord, and while they wait there in worship and faith, to experience the renewal of those spiritual powers upon which everything depends.

"And yet so frequently it happens that in ecclesiastical and theological gatherings, the so-called ordinary business occupies the first place, while hardly any time can be found for spiritual matters. And though we listened with great pleasure to what was said about the exercise of the spirit of love, about faithfulness to the doctrine of the church, and about the earnestness displayed in the council, more than one of us felt this great lack. I have no doubt that this lack will make itself felt even more in the future. . . ." Andrew's comment is as valid in today's ecclesiastical circles and gatherings as it was one hundred years ago, to the spiritual poverty of God's Kingdom.

Andrew attributed to the influence of Moody the fact that even in Scotland and England there was much more readiness now to speak out about one's religion and much more warmth. "I had noticed that the whole religious tone of Scotland has been lifted up and brightened most remarkably. I do praise God for it. Then, too, there is much earnest work being done, though I get the impression in many places that the activity and joy of *work* is regarded too much as the essence of religion. And I see that when I try to speak of the deeper and inner life, many are glad to listen, and confess to a want.

"For myself, I have learned this lesson, that it will not do to press too much on the one side of holiness and communion with Jesus, without the other side of work. There is no joy like that over repentant sinners, no communion closer than 'Go into all the world and teach — and lo! I am with you.' And yet the joy of work and of revival is *not* enough. God's children must be led into the secret of the *possibility of unbroken communion* with Jesus personally. I have been much impressed with the need of the union of these two matters, work and communion. . . ." And this point is truly what much of Andrew's writing was about — the balance between abiding and working, the inner life coupled with the outer service. Andrew exemplified both in his life.

After a rather restful voyage home, Andrew jumped right into work connected with his growing church, the Huguenot Seminary, the new Training Institute, the dispersing of the new teachers, and synodical matters, which combined projects would heavily tax the strength of any man. But at this time of his life Andrew was at the height of his powers of body and brain; his clear and ready mind and quick grasp of guiding principles enabled him to carry out with ease duties that others would scarcely attempt. He was impelled by the assurance that he was about his Father's business and his Father would enable him to carry it out.

16

Winds of Revival Blow South

Whatever winds were blowing on the European continent and in America, whether intellectual, religious or political, could not help but affect the younger, developing countries, including South Africa. Most of its influential class were academically prepared in those countries; books and magazines flowed from abroad to shape the public mind. Holland, Scotland and England, especially, deeply influenced the church life and thought.

The Dutch Reformed Church was by far the largest of the denominations in South Africa, with three times as many members as all other Protestant bodies combined. Since it had been freed of its governmental bondage of the early days, many new activities were begun and growth was significant.

Without question, Andrew Murray was the chief and most honored teacher of the Dutch Reformed Church. In whatever direction he grew in the Lord, whatever truths he grasped from the Word of God and taught, these spread throughout the church. As he formulated his own impressions for his study on what some people called the "higher life," others were drawn on. However, he was not without criticism and opposition even from his fellow pastors.

Andrew was continually growing deeper in the Lord, both in his practical experience and teaching concerning the life of sanctification. He was disappointed that in the Scotland of 1877 so few ministers had advanced beyond teaching elementary truths of the Lord. He felt that Christians in general were "terribly afraid of perfectionism." Entire consecration was a point he sought to emphasize. Conferences were springing up, some with Andrew's backing, not only for evangelism but for the deepening of the spiritual life of believers, even special conferences for ministers.

One such conference was held at Colesberg in 1879 expressly for the encouragement of ministers in their responsible spiritual tasks. Andrew underscored the value of such meetings in his invitation:

The blessing consists not merely in the interchange of thought, . . . the unity of the Spirit is also experienced more powerfully. [In this larger fellowship] the Spirit of God is found working with power, visions are instantaneously obtained which otherwise would only have come after the lapse of years, and we are strengthened to acts of faith and consecration for which we have longed for many months. . . . Solitude, however indispensable, is not sufficient. God speaks to *companies* of men as He never speaks to *solitary* watchers or students; there is a fuller tone, an intenser fervor, in pentecostal revelations [to a whole body] than in personal communion, and there is a keener joy [in group fellowship] than can be realized in the devoutest solitude.

The theme of that conference was "Enduring Joy," and the possibility of living always in such a spiritual communion with the Lord as to foster it. However, not all of the ministerial brethren present were convinced that such a life of faith, and such undisturbed peace and joy *were* really attainable, feeling it too ideal. As they studied together, it was brought out that such a life, "although high, was already known to the saints under the old dispensation, and therefore must surely be attainable by saints under the new." The realization of this truth led to more prayer."

Not only were Andrew's teachings on the deeper life not immediately accepted by fellow ministers, but they came under attack in the denominational magazine, in a "readers write" sort of debate. His own congregation was closely observed in order to discover whether his *higher teachings* were exemplified in their *higher conduct*. Critics were quick to jump on any discrepancies and enemies were ready to attack. Especially was his church watched to see if the members' financial giving was in line with their supposedly generous giving of themselves to the Lord in entire consecration. Andrew's congregation stood up well under this fire.

Great revivals were stirring other countries during this period. D. L. Moody and Ira D. Sankey strongly influenced Great Britain on their remarkable evangelistic trip across the Atlantic. Simple, untheologically educated laymen, they drew immense crowds; thousands were converted, believers were edified, churches were built up, and most remarkable, their unorthodox methods of work were accepted by many who were before most conservative and traditional.

These men never visited South Africa but the spiritual waves which they stirred up broke in force upon her shores. News of their campaigns hit the newspapers and magazines regularly; descriptions of their meetings and the results were common conversation everywhere. Persons who returned from Europe or America gave firsthand accounts of the new warmth and glow that so many hearts were experiencing. A spirit of high expectancy and prayer arose that God could and would do a similar work among His people anywhere.

And He did! Revivals broke out in Swellendam, Montagu, Wellington, Cape Town and Stellenbosch. A striking result was the large number of young people who were converted. Special campaigns were arranged by the synod to follow up these young people and conserve the results. Andrew was heavily engaged in such meetings and was freed by his church for several evangelistic tours within his country.

These "special services," as they were referred to, were not heretofore common in the Dutch Reformed Church; meetings were usually only in direct connection with local congregations. Andrew spent considerable time explaining and writing about their purpose in order to prevent misunderstanding, and to gain cooperation.

He assured the people, "No new gospel is being preached ... but these meetings are to preach solely the message of conversion and faith and to insist on the immediate acceptance of the Lord Jesus as Saviour. . . . It is always time to repent and believe but there are times when the minister seeks to insist with special earnestness upon *today* and *now.* The purpose of special services is nothing else than to shout this *now* in the sinner's ears."

While putting strong emphasis upon the cooperation of churches and Christians in these services — their preparation, visitation, assistance in counseling, and personal witness — Andrew underscored, *"Everything depends upon the Spirit of God* and the measure of faith in which His power is entreated and expected. . . . Present yourselves to Jesus Christ for His work, that He may gird you about with His Holy Spirit. . . . Encourage each other to expect great things. Continue steadfastly in secret and united prayer, and see if He will not open to you the windows of heaven and pour you out a blessing so that there shall not be room enough to receive it. . . ."

One of Andrew's trips lasted for two months and meetings were held in ten cities. The spiritual results of this series of special services in the wake of the revivals were great and permanent. The work was especially blessed among the children and the youth, not only in the villages and cities but in the different wards of the congregations. The young people often started weekly prayer meetings of their own and were greatly in earnest.

The congregation at Colesberg reported, ". . . indeed we have cause to shout. 'The Lord hath done great things for us, whereof we are glad.' Believers have been quickened and strengthened; the indifferent have been aroused and brought to Christ. Youth and age rejoice together in a new-found salvation."

And from another report: "Attendance was large beyond expectations. . . . Many can say, 'I have been anointed with fresh oil.' Even more noticeable is the blessing in the cases of many who have surrendered themselves to the Lord. . . . The good work is still proceeding quietly in our midst. We expect more blessing. The river of God is full of water!"

17

Made Perfect in Weakness

"Stop preaching at once!"

Such an order from Andrew's doctor must have been a great shock and test to the untiring, fiery minister. During the constant preaching in his own church and on extended tours for special services for evangelism and missions, it was normal for him to speak several times a day, and often he traveled far into the night to reach the next destination.

"I have first to fulfill the speaking engagements to which I am committed," argued Andrew.

"If you do, the condition will become far more serious. You will lose your voice altogether," insisted the doctor.

Because he did not immediately heed the warning, from 1879 he lost his voice for nearly two years, and was under strict orders to speak as little as possible, and only in a whisper. He stayed awhile with his brother-in-law to escape the kind inquiries made by visitors, and to see if the dry Karroo air would help him while he was under the care of an able doctor there. He saw the doctor once a day to have his throat treated, and twice a day for ten minutes he had to inhale steam with medicine mixed into it. He spent much of his time alone in his room or in the garden.

"The doctor says that he cannot say anything positive," wrote Andrew to his wife. "Not even to say there is any possibility of a cure. I enjoy the quiet and have not yet found time hanging heavy upon me." He used his time writing regularly for a Christian magazine, and producing tracts and booklets of a devotional nature. He made notes for the daily readings of the Bible and Prayer Union which he had just started. "With the cooperation of others, these notes may perhaps someday come to something." He added, "I have done a good deal of study, and taken up the reading again of McCheyne's life with much profit."

Andrew could not keep away from certain conferences in Montagu and Worcester, where he was to have delivered important messages. These had to be read to the assembled brethren. Nor was he able to address the synod meeting in Cape Town as retiring moderator; he was given a standing ovation of respect and gratitude for his services at that ceremony, though he could take no other active part.

Why did God allow or ordain that such a faithful servant as Andrew Murray should be set aside from preaching? The question must have been on the hearts if not on the lips of countless friends, co-workers and family. Of course Andrew himself had been facing it in the depths of his own spirit. He was only in his fifty-first year at the time.

He wrote to his wife, "My thoughts have been a good deal on the question of God's purpose for this long silence enforced upon me. You know what I have previously said about the two views of affliction: the one, that it is in chastisement for sin; the other, that it is in the light of the kindness and love of God. I have felt that it was a very great kindness to have such a time for the renewal of my bodily strength and of mental quiet and refreshment for the work before me.

"The thought has come, however, whether I might not be in danger of overlooking the former aspect. I have been asking the Lord to show me what specially there is that He wants changed in my life. The general answer is a very easy one, and yet it is difficult to realize at once distinctly where and how the change is to come. What is needed is a more spiritual life, more of the power of the Holy Ghost, in the life first, and then in the preaching. And yet it looks as if one's life is very much of a settled thing, and as if there is not much prospect of one's being lifted to a different platform. If the Holy Spirit were to come in great power to search and expose either my individual failings or the general low state of devotion in my soul, this would be the first step toward forsaking what is behind. Let us pray earnestly that our gracious God would search and try us and see whether there be any evil way in us. . . ."

During a visit to his childhood home at Graaff-Reinet, he stayed with his brother Charles who had taken his father's place as pastor. Charles apparently issued a brief medical bulletin to a Christian magazine that did not hint of any improvement in Andrew's condition. This worried Emma and the whole congregation at Wellington.

In comment, Andrew wrote his wife, "I'm sorry you were troubled about that notice, but it is simply the fact. . . . When people ask if I feel better, I never say yes, for I feel no difference. I have never written anything about being or feeling better. . . . I do not like to bother my doctor with questions about how long he thinks it may be until recovery. . . ."

Not long after that, Andrew reported that the doctor felt it would not be advisable to continue the silver nitrate treatments of his throat, but suggested that gentle and gradual exercise of the voice might be the next step, gradually to read or speak aloud in a room, later to give short addresses, slowly uttered. That was good news, and was followed later with his report that he preached for twenty-five minutes and the doctor said it had done him no harm. A huskiness persisted that was expected to wear off. He had already spent nearly a year and a half in silence.

But the sovereign God had been working a perfect plan which did not allow for unexpected detours. While unable to speak, Andrew naturally turned to more intensive writing, for which he might not have had much time if he had continued in his ever-accelerating preaching schedule.

"I have been getting on quite nicely with my writing. Strange that I marked out in a manuscript book the plan of a book some ten or twelve years ago, and that it should all at once flow from my pen so easily. Writing makes me wonder at our slowness of growth." He completed in the next few months his new book in Dutch, the original of *Like Christ*, and issued his first venture in English, *Abide in Christ*, which had previously been issued in Dutch. "I feel a little nervous about my debut in English!" he remarked.

He gradually resumed his preaching and returned to Wellington to hold services during Pentecost for the concerns of missions, which lay so near to his heart. His congregation responded with a large sum for missions and for the Missionary Training Institute in gratitude to God for their pastor's restoration to health.

However, the rejoicing was premature; Andrew suffered a considerable setback in the condition of his throat after that, so serious that he was advised to undertake a tour of Europe for a complete change of air and scene and to consult the best medical opinion. Emma accompanied him.

God had already been working in Andrew's heart previous to his voyage to consider the question of healing by faith. He had read, though without any particular conviction, a book by an American, Dr. W. E. Boardman, titled *The Lord Thy Healer.* There had also been certain meetings held in South Africa by a proponent of divine healing, and articles had appeared in a Christian magazine by this minister, Rev. Willem Hazenberg.

Hazenberg's position was that the diseases of believers must be regarded as judgments of God; God desires to remove instantly, by believing prayers, the diseases from which believers suffer. His ideas were strongly challenged, especially his first assertion. But many sincerely followed his teachings and he was in great demand in all parts of the country to lay hands upon the sick and pray for their recovery.

Andrew stated his beginning position in letters from Europe to his congregation, and continued to communicate with them how the Lord was leading him further as he inquired of God whether he did, indeed, have more to learn from the Word on God's perfect will for the health of His children.

"I had already given much thought to James 5:14-16 and together with others had already made this matter of faith healing a subject of intercession. I had no doubt that the Lord even yet bestows healing on the prayer of faith. And yet it was as though I could not reach that faith. Facing this trip to Europe, I felt I had to make a critical decision: should I turn myself over to a doctor to treat me, or should I turn *exclusively* to those who appear to have received this gift of healing from the Lord? I thought I'd made this decision while on board, but it was not settled."

Andrew most wanted to see Pastor Stockmaier, whom he had met some years before, a truly spiritual man, and at that time the head of an institute for faith healing in Switzerland. But he didn't expect to meet him until later. Meanwhile, upon landing, he placed himself in the hands of a famous London physician who prescribed some medicines and treatment and continued consultation. A week later, Andrew was slated to attend a Christian conference, where, to his surprise, Pastor Stockmaier was also present.

"I called on him and discussed my problem and my secret doubt that it may not be God's will that I should be healed. Rather, I countered, wouldn't it give God greater glory if I remained silent and served God in some other capacity? Surely suffering and trial are means of grace which God uses to sanctify His people."

Pastor Stockmaier replied to Andrew, "You are still fettered by the customary views of Christians about suffering. Observe how carefully James distinguishes in verses thirteen and fourteen between suffering and disease." He and Andrew most diligently went over the exegesis of that passage, with the result that Andrew himself saw quite clearly that there was no unconditional promise that suffering, arising from the many temptations and trials of life, would be taken away, nor should we pray to that end; but that there *is* such promise in the case of *sickness*, and *that* we should claim.

"I understand the matter better. Suffering that comes upon the Christian from the world without must serve to bless and sanctify him. But it is different with disease, which has its origin within the body, not outside of it. The body has been redeemed; it is the temple of the Holy Spirit; and for the believer who can accept it, the Lord is ready to reveal even in the case of the body, His mighty power to deliver from the dominion of sin."

Pastor Stockmaier invited Andrew to attend the meetings of the Dr. Boardman whose book about healing Andrew had read before coming to Europe. Dr. Boardman had written another book, *The Higher Christian Life*, and had opened another institute for faith healing, called Bethshan, right in London. Andrew visited it and felt clearly led to ask to be received as a patient; he remained there for three weeks.

"I imagine you may wonder why it was necessary to enter a special place and remain there for so long a time," Andrew wrote to his congregation. "You may think that surely the prayer of faith is a matter of a moment, just like the laying on of hands or the anointing with oil of which James speaks. Quite true. Yet in most cases, time is needed in order to learn what God's Word actually promises and to rightly understand what the cause and purpose of the disease really are, and what are the conditions and the meaning of healing.

Remaining in such a home, with all its surroundings, helps to make this matter plain and to strengthen faith."

Andrew described what went on as a daily schedule there: "Morning by morning, sixteen or eighteen of us who sought healing were gathered around the Word of God and instructed as to what still remained in us to prevent us from appropriating the promise, and what there was in Scripture to encourage us to faith and to complete surrender. I cannot remember that I ever listened to expositions of the Word of God in which greater simplicity and a more glorious spirit of faith were revealed, combined with heart-searching application of God's demand to surrender everything to Him."

And then there were times of private prayers and counseling with Pastor Stockmaier. "When he prayed with me the first time, he used the expression of 1 Corinthians 11:31,32, 'Lord, teach him to judge himself, that he may no longer be judged or chastened.' I find there the main thoughts concerning sickness and cure. In what way is sickness a chastisement? Because God judges us in love so that we may not be condemned with the world. If we judge ourselves in such a manner as to discover the reason for which we are being chastised, then, so soon as the reason is removed the chastisement itself is no longer necessary. The disease was designed to bring us to complete severance from what God disapproved of in our life; when the Lord has attained this purpose, the disease itself may be removed.

"Must these be definite sins, you may inquire? Sometimes, though not always. They may be a lack of complete consecration, the assertion of one's own will, confidence in one's own strength in performing the Lord's work, a forsaking of one's first love and tenderness in the walk with God, or the absence of that gentleness which desires to follow only the leading of the Spirit of God.... Our surrender to the Holy Spirit as we ask for healing is to express our readiness to live every day in complete dependence upon the Lord for our bodily welfare. . . . The Lord, in thus giving and preserving health by faith, is really effecting the most intimate union with Himself."

Andrew made it clear that the believer who was healed was not to accept his healing and run, so to speak, considering it an accomplished fact of the past and going on as before. He emphasized that a healing was meant to establish or re-establish a permanent, vital, moment-by-moment union with the Lord, in order to maintain that new infusion of health.

Andrew knew whereof he spoke, for he was indeed *healed by the Lord* during his stay at the Bethshan Home, so completely that never again was he troubled by any weakness of throat or voice. He depended constantly upon the Lord for its use for the rest of his life. In spite of the heavy strain imposed on it, his voice retained its strength till his eighty-eighth year, with a clear, youthful, musical, and penetrating quality which surprised many. Those who heard him for the first time did not expect such a voice to issue from so frail and aged a body.

"Some object to, even shun, the possibility of healing, because they think that disease and chastisement bring *blessing.* Do you not realize that recovery brings even *greater* blessing? When the healing has brought about a closer contact with the living Lord, and a more complete union of the body with Him, then we can understand that such a recovery does bring infinitely greater blessing to the soul than the disease could convey," he explained.

Before Andrew had left South Africa, his state of health was so poor that a nephew wrote to his parents, "Uncle Andrew is very ill. You had better come and say good-bye (permanently) to him before he goes to England." Now Andrew returned to the ministry in full vigor. Not only so, but there was a noticeable change of manner in his dealings with people, an even deeper launching out into a walk in the Spirit, and a difference in tone in his preaching. God had brought him through another sovereignly planned step of growth, so that he might teach others.

His eldest daughter described the change in her father perceptively: "It was after the 'time of silence' when God came so near to Father and he saw more clearly the meaning of a life of full surrender and simple faith, that he began to show in all relationships that constant tenderness and unruffled lovingkindness and unselfish thought for others which increasingly characterized his life from that point. At the same time he lost nothing of his strength and determination.

"More and more was developed that wonderful, grave, and beautiful humility which could never be put on, but could only be the work of the indwelling Spirit. It was felt immediately by all who came into contact with him."

He had been sober and even severe during his overwhelming responsibilities in the early days of his work in the Orange Free State and Transvaal. He had then dealt severely with himself and felt the need for strict discipline toward his people. This was in great contrast to his natural temperament, for when he first returned to South Africa as a young minister, straight from college, he was overflowing with fullness of life and merriment. But underneath he was always the same man, serious and yearning after the fullness of God, ever surrendering himself more completely to his Lord, but maturing and mellowing as he became more attuned to the Spirit. God invested eighty-eight years to work in Andrew Murray the image and likeness of his adorable Master and Lord.

18

The Afterward of Healing

Andrew's new faith in God's healing power was tested as soon as he arrived home. The Murrays had left their younger children in the care of Miss McGill, an old friend of the family. She had become seriously ill during their absence and met them with, "I have lived just long enough to deliver the children to you again."

"Oh, no," said Andrew. "God still needs you in South Africa and He will restore you in answer to prayer; though doctors despair, there is hope in the Lord who heals us."

Then he explained to her the principles of faith healing and offered earnest prayer for her recovery. She was doubtful at first, but before long she stepped out on faith for her healing, regained strength, rose up from her sick bed and was restored to labor for many years in the Y.W.C.A. of Cape Town.

The subject of the Lord's healing was a vital part of Andrew's ministry from that point forward. In 1884 he published in Dutch a book titled *Jesus, the Physician of the Sick*. He acknowledged that many objections may be leveled at faith healing to which no satisfactory answer at present can be found. But he stated that his aim was not so much to meet objections as to attempt an exposition of what Scripture taught on the subject.

This book was later published in French and in English under the title *Divine Healing*, which Andrew much preferred. The connotations of the term "faith healing" might be construed to take in many philosophies which were not even Christian. But Andrew, and those from whom he learned these truths, understood that it is not *faith* that heals, but faith is the hand that *receives* the gift from the *Healer*, who is God.

Let us ask Andrew more about his position on healing. (His answers are taken verbatim from his book *Divine Healing*.)

Were not the miracles and gifts of the Spirit only for the apostolic Church?

"Basing my views on Scripture, I do *not* believe that miracles and the other gifts of the Spirit were limited to the time of the primitive Church, nor that their object was to establish the foundation of Christianity and then disappear by God's withdrawal of them."

Why do we see them, including healing, so little today?

"Because the Church has become so worldly that the Spirit can act but feebly in her."

Can we expect to see more miracles today?

"If the Church were to see anew springing up within her, men and women who live the life of faith and of the Holy Spirit, entirely consecrated to their God, we would see again the manifestation of the same gifts as in former times. . . . *The Church must expect great outpourings of the Spirit in these days*, and may reckon upon this gift [of healing] likewise."

Is there any limitation to Mark 16:17,18 about the signs which Jesus said would follow those that believe?

"The Bible does not authorize us, either by the words of the Lord or His apostles, to believe that the gifts of healing were granted only to the early times of the Church; on the contrary, the promise of Jesus to the apostles when He gave them instructions concerning their mission, shortly before His ascension, appear to us *applicable to all times*. Paul places the gift of healing among the operations of the Holy Spirit. James gives a precise command on this matter *without restriction of time*. The entire Scriptures declare that these graces will be granted according to the measure of the Spirit and of faith."

Were not miracles much more necessary in the early days of Christianity than later?

"Ah no. What about the power of heathenism even today wherever the gospel seeks to combat it, even in our *modern* society, and in the midst of the ignorance and unbelief which reigns even in the Christian nations?"

"I had certain questions myself at the beginning of my search for God's truth in the matter of healing," admitted Andrew. One was: "Why, in many cases, is slow progress made with the healing process? If it is an act of God's almighty power, why is everyone not perfected *at once?*"

It was Dr. Boardman who helped him to a satisfactory answer. "Many times such gradual recovery brings about a learning to trust in the Lord and to continue in *constant* dependence upon Him. God is often educating His child to the increasing exercise of faith and to a continuance of communion with Himself."

Dr. Stockmaier reinforced this answer with his own experience of being wholly incapacitated from preaching for more than two years with a problem in his head. The trouble did not disappear even after he had accepted the truth of healing, though he was always able to perform his work in the power of fellowship with the Lord by faith.

"He assured me," said Andrew, "that he would not for all the world have exchanged for an immediate recovery what he learned during those two years of *gradual* healing."

"But I still had the question," wrote Andrew, "of whether an instantaneous and complete healing would not be a much more powerful proof, both for Christians and for the world at large, and bring more glory to God."

The answer which satisfied Andrew immediately was, "The Lord knows better than you what is for His greater glory. *Leave it to Him* to care for His own glory. Your duty is to hold fast to Him as your Healer, in whom you already have your healing, and He will enable you, in such manner as He sees fit, to perform all your work."

It is apparent from an interview between Andrew and one of his colleagues, Rev. J. R. Albertyn, that he never supported the dictum that "all disease has its source in the devil." He himself wrote that the sick were not more sinful than the sound; and from his book *Divine Healing* it is also apparent that he held that the divine mystery of the answer to prayer applied also to healing by faith.

Andrew had observed instantaneous healings, both while he was under instruction at Bethshan and in subsequent years through his own ministry. God's sovereignty binds Him only to do His work perfectly, with whatever variety He sees best.

"A girl at Bethshan had suffered for years from many diseases, epilepsy among others, and several doctors declared that nothing could be done for her. She lay half conscious on the sofa during the prayer meetings. Prayer continued on her behalf, until one day when it seems that she suddenly grasped the full truth of Isaiah 53. She immediately rose and said, 'If Christ *has borne* my sicknesses, I need not *carry* them any longer.' And within a short time she was completely cured." Andrew declared that on subsequent occasions he himself heard her bear witness with great joy to the Lord's healing.

So convinced had Andrew become of the Lord's power to heal that he wondered, "whether I may not perhaps possess the gift of healing, and have the vocation, and should devote myself, for a time at least, to this work. I notice in those who are engaged in this healing ministry that they must give almost all their time and strength to it so that their faith acquires sufficient vitality and strength to enable them to wrestle courageously with all the doubts and difficulties of their patients."

He consulted several mature Christian leaders who gave him the advice that *not everyone who had been healed* was to devote himself to the vocation of healing others. Each one must wait for the Lord's guidance to assign his work according to his ability and God's plan. It was Samuel Zeller who reminded him that for some the ministry of the gospel might be a higher vocation. At the same time, within the church and the leadership of the congregation, indeed among the ministers themselves, the gift of healing should be found very much more frequently as believers move more deeply in the Holy Spirit. Andrew found this remarkably true in the years to come as he ministered both the gospel and the healing teaching in the ordinary opportunities the Lord set before him.

Andrew apparently never receded from the position on divine healing to which he felt the Lord had led him through the study of Scripture and his personal experience. It was not true that Andrew was henceforth never sick, weak, or without accident. Nor was it true that each case for which he prayed for healing recovered. There were some outstanding cases where much prayer was made, and much faith exercised, and the believers still died. Several of his pastor friends and his own family members were among these, the young and dedicated as well as the old. Although Andrew himself did not understand why, in these cases, God did not heal, and could not explain it to others, yet it did not shake his faith that God *can* and *does* and *will* heal, subject to His sovereignty, and that believers ought to obey Him and continue to ask in faith.

Did Andrew cease consulting doctors after he had found new faith in God as the Healer? It is recorded that for the sake of easing the minds of relatives and friends, he did not refuse, as a rule, to see the doctor if they persisted.

"We may be thankful to God for giving us doctors," he wrote. "Their vocation is one of the most noble; a larger number of them seek truly to do, with love and compassion, all they can to alleviate the evils and sufferings which burden humanity as a result of sin. Some are zealous servants of Jesus Christ who seek also the good of their patients' souls.

"Nevertheless, it is Jesus Himself who is always the first, the best, the greatest Physician. Jesus heals diseases in which earthly physicians can do nothing, for the Father gave Him this power when He charged Him with the work of our redemption. . . . Even in our day, how many have been given up by the doctors as incurable; how many cases of cancer, infection, paralysis, heart disease, blindness, and deafness have been healed by Him! Is it not then astonishing that so small a number of the sick *apply to Him?*"

There were times, however, when Andrew felt he should cast himself upon the Great Physician alone. In 1907, already at an advanced age, he suffered from a severe attack of the flu, and it appeared that he might die from it.

His daughter described the situation: "Father was very ill and my mother was quite broken-hearted and asked me, 'What am I to do?' I went to Father and said, 'Father, dear, which will you do: have the doctor or have someone anoint you and pray with you?'

"Father said, 'I will have *neither,* my child. You can hold as many prayer meetings as you like, but *I will trust in God!*'

"I went out and arranged for three different meetings to pray for his restoration to health. To the praise of God, Father preached the next Sunday, fully recovered, a most remarkable sermon on the text, 'They limited the Holy One of Israel' (Psalm 78:41). Once more Father proved the faithfulness of God!"

When traveling in Natal on one of his evangelistic tours, the cart in which he was riding upset, he was thrown out, and his arm was visibly broken. He bandaged it himself as well as he could, applying cold water compresses, and preached that evening as usual. The broken arm was made a matter of prayer and so complete was the healing that some months later when Andrew showed it to a doctor friend, the doctor assured him that it had been "most remarkably and perfectly set and healed."

Some years later, Andrew and Emma were both thrown again from a cart on a similar tour into northern Transvaal, and he was seriously hurt in the leg and back. This time relatives insisted on calling a doctor, and though he did not give up his tour, he was never perfectly restored and had to forgo ever traveling by cart again.

His wife, like himself, was strongly convinced of the truth of divine healing and supported him in his ministry among the sick. Emma preceded him in death, by eleven years, of a sudden illness, for which they undoubtedly beseeched the Lord with earnest prayers of faith. But neither was unrealistic in deceiving himself that there was no *natural end* to life on this earth, but recognized that earthly tabernacles do get worn out by use and time. God has new bodies for His children, ready to be exchanged for their old ones, bodies which will last for all eternity.

And so it was that when his own fullness of time arrived to lay aside his tent of eighty-eight years, there was no disappointment that he was not healed, but a joyful, peaceful acceptance of the providence of God and of the timing of his promotion to Glory.

His daughter who cared for him in his last years comments that when Andrew had to be confined to bed on doctor's orders, no patient was more obedient to instructions, more cheerful in attitude, or more grateful for the least attention.

She wrote about Andrew's attitude toward not receiving healing from that cart accident: "One cool evening I was sitting with my father on the veranda and he said to me in his humble way, 'My child, I would so much like to hold evangelistic meetings but God does not see fit to heal me.' He sighed a little as he said this, and I felt it was a mystery that at the very time God was using him so mightily as a soul winner, this accident should have happened. But it proved to be his Peniel. He became, through this experience, a prince who prevailed with God in an even greater way in prayer. He was led through this seemingly strange providence into an even deeper prayer life, and was taught what the power of intercession really was.

"His remarkable books on prayer were all written *after* that accident, and the influence they have exercised cannot be measured by man. God glorified Himself in His servant, and in spite of his lameness, he lived to a good old age, and at last sweetly fell asleep in Jesus — 'A shock of corn fully ripe.' "

19

Personal Testimony

"Why don't you write an autobiography, Mr. Murray, especially to trace your spiritual development?"

Many were the people of influence who urged this upon him. Dr. Alexander Whyte was so intensely anxious that Andrew should give to the world such a work that he said it would be the one book that he wished to read before he passed away.

He even went so far as to send a note to his own publisher with a prospective title for Andrew's autobiography and put the notation "In Preparation" on it. But to no avail.

Andrew maintained that his own spiritual experiences were not sufficiently clear-cut. On one occasion his daughter brought up the subject again while Andrew was selecting quotations from William Law for one of his booklets.

"Well," he said, "if I could pass through Law's experiences, I might be persuaded to set down something, but not otherwise."

When she suggested that his own experiences may have been equally deep and vivid, though not necessarily along the same lines as Law's, he shook his head and said, "No, my child. God has been very gracious to me; but in this matter I must have something more to go upon before I can venture to write." He persisted in this humble refusal to the end, and the world saw no autobiography of Andrew Murray.

We must be content to trace his spiritual pilgrimage through the outward events of his life, his burdens and concerns, his preaching and teaching themes, and the topics of his writings. As we note the stages of Andrew's life in the foregoing, we glean something of his spiritual development. In this biography we have been observing successive changes and areas of his increasing maturity. If we are alert, we can put the pieces together.

It is true, as Andrew declared, that his testimony was not really systematic; therefore he felt that his spiritual development should not be taken as a pattern for all believers. We will honor that. Indeed, no one's life, no matter how prominent a Christian leader, should be taken as an ultimate pattern. All of God's children are still in process at any given period of their lives. God is continuing to work in them through their particular circumstances to shape them into the image of His Son.

In the same way, no one has yet attempted a systematic study of Andrew Murray's theology. The question arises whether this does not bear witness to the depth of his teachings. Still less have his biographers succeeded in fixing upon the exact secret of his spiritual influence. Once again, this may be because of the inadequacy of any human scale of values by which to assess his life and work, or perhaps because his influence was like the atmosphere — essential and beneficial, but defying analysis and definition.

In this chapter we shall attempt to pick up some important pieces, heretofore missing, to round out as much as we can the portrayal of Andrew's spiritual development. Let us watch for the broad sweep and not stumble at the details.

Andrew's manner of preaching was, from the beginning, very distinctive. Upon returning as a young preacher from Scotland, he was often asked to preach in his father's church. The sexton always wanted to be alerted beforehand. "If Mr. Andrew preaches, I must remove the lamps, for in his fiery zeal they will be in his way."

This characteristic marked his preaching all his life. Even in later years, some of his hearers noted with interest the clouds of dust which rose from pounding the pulpit cushion when he began his sermon; but before it was finished, they noted that the dusting had been completed. Andrew was never violent or unrestrained, only glowing with intensity.

Despite his early zeal, Andrew was always spiritually discontented and reaching forward. "Ministerial responsibilities begin to press increasingly heavily upon me," he wrote early in his career. "Oh, how easy and content have I been living while souls have been perishing. How little have I felt the compassion with which Christ was moved when He wept over sinners. Oh! I feel it is not enough to be faithful in speaking the truth — the minister's spirit is something very different. Love to souls so filling our hearts that we cannot rest because of them, would lead us to be very different from what we are. While I have been abundant in external labors —

oh! — yet I have felt nothing of that 'the zeal of thine house hath consumed me.' I trust that the Lord is, however, leading me to more earnestness in prayer — though I feel if He keep me not, my reluctant flesh is every moment ready to say 'It is enough.' "

He wrote later, "Most cordially do I sympathize with Papa in the wishes he expresses for the Spirit to be granted in connection with our preaching. And yet, I do not know what hampers me so dreadfully in striving to believe in prayer or even to pray earnestly. I fear it is because my religion is as yet very much a selfish thing . . . . If my *own* soul be safe, or if *my* ministry be blessed, or if *our* church might be revived — this is too much yet the only motive in prayer. . . .

"As yet my prayers are not such as will draw down blessing. But it may be that God will give it of His great mercy. . . . I often enjoy much peace and happiness, but lest I should be exalted, the thorn in the flesh and the messenger of Satan is not wanting." Andrew pinpointed for us what he believed that thorn was: " . . . the fearful outbreak of my pride and self-esteem."

It seems that Andrew recognized the insidious danger of popularity and being well spoken of even in the context of the ministry. Everywhere he went he was acclaimed and praised. Even as a young man he realized that was not to his advantage. "At moments I feel dissatisfied, then again very earnest, but still I fear there is at the root a secret feeling that I could be worse, and that there are many a great deal worse. . . .

"I thought I hated the name of being very diligent and earnest in the work of God — and yet my deceitful heart has not failed to appropriate a portion of the praise for the satisfaction of my own vanity. . . . I seem to have a secret self-complacency.... Why has the Lord put me in the ministry — so unfit as I am — leaving me to wrestle with the awful work in my own impotence? Oh! why can I not find the needful strength?"

In reflecting upon his condition later, he wrote, "I have thought much of the text, 'If ye abide in me, ye shall ask what ye will.' A man can't accomplish his work if his strength is not daily maintained by eating. So it is only a daily living on Christ that can make us strong for the great work of interceding for sinners. . . .Oh! for holier lives, more of the felt power of an indwelling Saviour, more living participation in the new life, and the power revealed in the resurrection of our Jesus." By allowing him to taste unvictorious living, God was seeding His servant Andrew for the writing of a simple book which has changed the lives of countless saints: *Abide in Christ.*

Andrew seldom gave what we would consider a personal testimony in his messages or in his writings. He remarked to a friend of the family once that some people objected to his reluctance. But that friend replied, "I think that the great power in your books consists of *just that* — that there is so little of yourself in them and Christ is always in the foreground."

"Mr. Murray, won't you make an exception and share *just a little* with us of your own spiritual pilgrimage from the beginning until now?" The request became insistent at a particular Keswick Convention in England. Andrew did make that exception by popular request, and shared, in much humility, some of God's dealings with him through the years. It was recorded in *The Christian* magazine of August 15, 1895. We consider it significant and precious because it is the only record of its kind. He was ever fearful of drawing the attention of his hearers from Christ to any experience.

When I was asked to give my testimony, I doubted whether it would be desirable, and for this reason: we all know what helpfulness there is in a clear-cut testimony of a man who can say: "There I was; I knelt down and God helped me and I entered into the better life." I cannot give such a testimony, but I know what blessing it has often brought to me to read of such testimonies for the strengthening of my own faith. And yet I got this answer from those who urged me to speak: "Perhaps there are many at Keswick to whom a testimony concerning a life of more struggle and difficulty will be helpful." If it must be so, I replied, let me tell for the glory of God how He has led me.

Some of you have heard how I press upon you the *two* stages in the Christian life, and the step from the one to the other. The first ten years of my spiritual life were manifestly spent on the lower stage. I was a minister, I may say, as zealous and as earnest and as happy in my work as anyone, as far as love of the *work* was concerned. Yet all the time there was burning in my heart a dissatisfaction and restlessness inexpressible. What was the reason? Although my justification was as clear as noonday, and I knew the hour in which I received from God the joy of pardon, I had never learned, with all my theology, that *obedience* was possible.

I remember (later) in my little room at Bloemfontein how I used to sit and ask, What is the matter? Here I am, knowing that God has justified me in the blood of Christ, but I have *no power for service*. My thoughts, my words, my actions, my unfaithfulness — everything troubled me. Though all around thought me to be one of the most earnest of men, my life was one of deep dissatisfaction. I struggled and prayed as best I could.

One day I was talking with a missionary. I do not think that he knew much of the power of sanctification himself — he would have admitted it. When we were talking and he saw my earnestness, he said, "Brother, remember that when God puts a desire into your heart, *He will fulfill it.*" That helped me; I thought of it a hundred times. I want to say the same to you who are plunging about and struggling in the quagmire of helplessness and doubt. The desire that God puts into your heart He will fulfill.

. . . If any are saying that God has not a place for them, let them trust God, and wait, and He will help you and show you what is your place. So the Lord led me until in His great mercy I had been eleven or twelve years in Bloemfontein. Then He brought me to another congregation in Worcester about the time when God's Holy Spirit was being poured out in America, Scotland, and Ireland. In 1860, when I had been six months in that congregation, God poured out His Spirit there in connection with my preaching, especially as I was moving about in the country, and a very unspeakable blessing came to me.

The first Dutch edition of my book *Abide in Christ* was written at that time. I would like you to understand that a minister or a Christian author may often be led to *say* more than he has *experienced*. I had *not* then experienced all that I wrote of; I cannot say that I experience it all perfectly even now.

Well, God helped me, and for seven or eight years I went on, always enquiring and seeking, and *always getting*. Then about 1870 came the great Holiness Movement. The letters that appeared in *The Revival* magazine touched my heart; and I was in close fellowship with what took place at Oxford and Brighton, and it *all* helped me.

Perhaps if I were to talk of consecration, I might tell you of a certain evening there in my own study in Cape Town. Yet I cannot say that *that* was my deliverance, for I was still struggling. Later on my mind became much exercised about the baptism of the Holy Spirit and I gave myself to God as perfectly as I could to receive the baptism of the Spirit. *Yet* there was failure; God forgive it. It was somehow as if I could not *get* what I wanted. Through all these stumblings God led me, without any very special experience that I can point to. But as I look back, I do believe now that He was giving me more and more of His blessed Spirit, had I but known it better.

I can help you more, perhaps, by speaking, not of any marked experience, but by telling very simply *what I think God has given me now,* in contrast to the first ten years of my Christian life.

In the first place, I have learned to place myself before God *every* day, as a vessel to be *filled* with His Holy Spirit. He has filled me with the blessed assurance that He, as the everlasting God, has guaranteed His own work in me. If there is one lesson that I am learning day by day, it is this: that it is *God who worketh all in all.* Oh, that I could help any brother or sister to realize this!

I was once preaching and a lady came to talk with me. She was a very pious woman, and I asked her, "How are you getting on?"

Her answer was, "Oh, just the way it always is, sometimes light and sometimes dark."

"My dear sister, where is *that* in the Bible?"

She said, "We have day and night in nature, and just so it is in our souls."

No, no! In the Bible we read, "Your sun shall *no more* go down." Let me believe that I am God's child, and that the Father in Christ, through the Holy Ghost, has set His love upon me, and that I may *abide* in His presence, not frequently, but *unceasingly.* The veil has been rent; the Holiest of all opened. By the grace of my God I have to take up my abode there, and there my God is going to teach me what I never could learn while I dwelt outside. My home is always in the abiding love of the Father in Heaven.

You will ask me, Are you satisfied? Have you *got all* you want? God forbid! With the deepest feeling of my soul I can say *I am satisfied with Jesus now;* but there is also the consciousness of *how much fuller* the revelation can be of the exceeding abundance of His grace. Let us never hesitate to say, This is only the *beginning.* When we are brought into the Holiest of all, we are only beginning to take our right position with the Father.

I will tell you where you probably fail. You have never yet heartily believed that *He is working out your salvation.* Of course you believe that if a painter undertakes a picture, he must look to every shade and color and every touch upon the canvas. You believe that if a workman makes a table or a bench, he knows how to do his work. But you do *not* believe that the everlasting God is in the process of working out the image of His Son in you. As any sister here is doing a piece of ornamental or fancy work, following out the pattern in every detail, let her just think: "Can God not work out *in me* the purpose of His love?" If that piece of work is to be perfect, every stitch must be in its place. So remember that *not one minute* of your life should be *without God.* We often want God to come in at a certain time — say in the morning; then we are content to live two or three hours on our own, and He then can come in again. No! God must be *every moment the Worker in your soul.*

It is no wonder, with a burning conviction like the above, that at those conventions Andrew was never weary of calling for the hymn with the refrain: "Moment by moment I'm kept in His love; Moment by moment

I've life from above; Looking to Jesus till glory ͏͏͏͏ ͏͏
shine; Moment by moment, O Lord, I am Thine."
Andrew concluded his testimony:

> May He teach us our own nothingness and
> transform us into the image of His Son and help
> us to go out to be a blessing to our fellow men.
> Let us trust Him and praise Him in the midst of a
> consciousness of failure and of a remaining
> tendency to sin. Notwithstanding this, let us
> believe that our God loves to *dwell in us;* and let
> us hope without ceasing in His *still more
> abundant* grace.

A further insight into the fact that Andrew was still
pressing on, and was open to being taught by others,
even while teaching others himself, is given in a letter to
his sister. Apparently she had written him that she
wished she could consult with some of the key persons of
the Holiness Movement, Mr. Robert Pearsall Smith or
Dr. Boardman, to ask them what was the secret of their
victory in the Christian life. Andrew answered that he
felt *he knew* what they would say, as he had discussed
that very point with them. He explained to his sister:

> Many felt as if the full baptism of the Spirit
> was lacking. The answers of these brethren all
> ran in one direction: You must trust Jesus in the
> assurance that He will make everything right *in
> due time.* You must really rest in Him as an all-
> sufficient portion. In your desires for more
> blessing, you must see that your joyful rest is not
> disturbed. The joyful, praising acknowledge-

ment that you *have* everything in Him, that unutterable fullness *dwells* and that you *are* complete in Him must not be dimmed by the desire for what you do not *yet* see or feel.

I spoke with a certain lady about it. She said that we must remember that there is a diversity of gifts and operations in different people and at different times. Mrs. Hannah Whithall Smith was still seeking for a baptism of the Spirit while everybody thought she already had it remarkably. It might be that we are mistaken in the idea we form of it. Experience, feeling, success are not given to all in the same degree.

At Mr. Moody's after-meeting where I had been helping, speaking to the spiritually anxious, God sent an old man to deal with *us*. He said, "Brothers, may I ask whether *you* enjoy the full rest?"

I gave an honest answer. In the course of conversation he said that such wishes may be a thought of the old nature leading me off from what I *am* in Christ — that I should say *at once* that I am dead to every such thought of discontent and dissatisfaction. The Holy Spirit who *has* been given me in His *fullness* is equal to every need and emergency.

I spoke about it with Mr. and Mrs. Palmer who have for forty years been holding Holiness meetings in their own home in New York. Mr. Palmer said, "It may be a temptation of Satan. If you *have truly surrendered everything*, you must beware of being led off from your faith in Jesus by what you *still seek* in your experience." And we had a very precious prayer meeting together.

And after a prayer meeting at Mrs. Keene's in Philadelphia, we had another talk. I spoke of the feeling I had that the blessing came more easily, while in fellowship with other believers. She said that she had more than once attended Holiness meetings and seen people attain experiences of which *she* could not speak. Sometimes people who were not very well prepared or whose surrender was not so deep or full as that of others, apparently got less of a blessing. Her chief thought, too, was that we should *maintain the assurance of our surrender* and our trust, and *then ask and expect more* with patience.

See there, my dearest Ellen, what I have been taught in America — if not in the words of the speakers, yet in substance. And I have taken the lesson to myself and am rejoicing and will rejoice whatever comes, because *Jesus Christ, the Living Saviour, is all I need!*

And you, too, should take this lesson and no more speak of the *feebleness* of your consecration. Our mistake is, I think, that *we form our own ideal* of an abiding exhibition of power and success which is *not* according to the mind of God. We *cannot* live so that *every* word we speak shall be blessed to the conversion of a soul, but we *can* live so that every word we speak shall be *to the glory of God* — spoken in quiet obedience and trust and then committed to Him who giveth the increase.

Interwoven in most of Andrew's teachings and writings is the concept of "holiness." It is important to know what position he took. He held that within the born-again Christian believer there does remain sinful tendency, but also held, as quite compatible with this, the possibility of a freedom from actual sinning. Holiness or perfection as applied to the believer does not mean that we *can no longer sin*, but that we are *able not to sin*.

Andrew defended it further: "It is a spiritual state which before death the sanctified can enter, and remain there until death. It is entered by the blood of Jesus applied through specific faith and by one definite, marked, and well-remembered crisis. Different terms may be applied to it, such as 'entire consecration,' or 'the baptism of the Spirit and fire,' or 'the fullness of faith,' etc. . . . God's plan is that *soon* after conversion, the sooner the better, we should enter into this Holiest of all."

The writer of one of Andrew's former biographies refers to a remarkable book, *Deeper Experiences of Famous Christians*, which documents accurately the experiences of Christians such as Madame Guyon, Fenelon, George Fox, Wesley, Whitefield, John Fletcher, Christmas Evans, William Bramwell, General Booth, Moody, Dr. A. J. Gordon, A. B. Earle, Frances Havergal and many others. Each of their testimonies includes a definite crisis experience that they had *after their conversion*. It was as marked in time as a birth or a death or a marriage, and by it they passed into a new state and experience, a new relation to Christ and the Holy Spirit and a new appropriation and application of the all-cleansing power of the Blood, not only to cleanse but to keep clean.

Such witnesses are certainly considered illustrious and reliable. Andrew warned of the danger in thinking that such experiences are *exceptional* and that holiness is *optional*. He said that the possibility argues its necessity; that it is *attainable* shows that it is *indispensable*.

20

Deeper Into Secrets

Did Andrew Murray feel that his teaching on the Holy Spirit was something new when viewed in the perspective of the historical Church and the finality of God's revelation in the Scriptures?

He explained it thus:

"It is generally admitted in the Church that the Holy Spirit has not the recognition which becomes Him as being the equal of the Father and the Son, the Divine Person through whom alone the Father and the Son can be truly possessed and known, in whom alone the Church has her beauty and her blessedness.

"In the Reformation, the *gospel* of Christ had to be vindicated from the terrible misapprehension which makes man's righteousness the ground of his acceptance, and the freeness of divine grace had to be maintained.

"To the ages that followed was committed the trust of building on that foundation, and developing what the riches of grace would do for the believer through the indwelling of the Spirit of Jesus. The Church rested too content in what it had received, and the teaching of all that the Holy Spirit will be to each believer in His guiding, sanctifying, strengthening power *has never yet taken the place it ought to have* in our evangelical teaching and living."

And then he quoted from a book, *The Lord's Prayer* by Saphir: "If we review the history of the Church, we notice how many important truths, clearly revealed already in Scripture, have been allowed to *lie dormant for centuries,* unknown and unappreciated except by a few isolated Christians, until it pleased God to enlighten the Church by chosen witnesses, and to bestow on His children the knowledge of hidden and forgotten treasures. For how long a period, even *after* the Reformation, were the doctrines of the *Holy Ghost,* His work in conversion, and His indwelling in the believer, *almost unknown!"*

God chose Andrew Murray as one of His spiritual miners to unearth some of the choicest of the "hidden and forgotten treasures" of the Holy Spirit to his generation, with the rich overflow to the generations that followed.

Andrew believed and taught, "There is such a thing as a Pentecost still, in the *personal experience* of the believer." The Holy Spirit, he believed, is the connecting and logical agent to undertake to communicate the holiness of Christ to us. The vital truth of the New Testament that the Christian is *holy in Christ* needs as its correlative that the *Holy One is in the Christian.* And the outcome of personal holiness must be active service for Christ in saving men.

In answer to what is meant by the baptism of the Holy Ghost and whether it is not merely a part of our initial experience of the new birth when He comes to indwell us, Andrew explained:

"The baptism of the Holy Ghost is the crown and glory of Jesus' work and we need it: we must *know* that we *have* it if we are to live the true Christian life. It is *more* than the Spirit's work in regeneration. It is the personal Spirit of Christ making Him present with us, always abiding in the heart in the power of His glorified nature. . . . To so many regenerate people this is only a blessing *registered* on their behalf, but *not possessed* or *enjoyed*. It is the enduement with power to fill us with boldness in the presence of every danger, and give the victory over every enemy.

"Whether we look upon this baptism as something we already have, or something we must receive, in this all agree, that it is only in the fellowship of Jesus, in faithful attachment and obedience to Him, that a baptized life can be *received*, or *maintained* or *renewed*. . . .The question is, do we know Him as the *Baptizer* imparting the Holy Ghost or only as the *Atoner*, the Lamb of God taking away the sin of the world?"

Andrew was not indistinct or ambiguous in his theology of the Holy Spirit, but was anchored firmly in the full context of Scripture at every point. He stated his teaching clearly in many of his books, but most specifically in *The Spirit of Christ* (even more in detail in the extensive notes comprising the last quarter of the book) and in his book *The Full Blessing of Pentecost*.

Drawing a few excerpts from the former book to spell out his convictions, we let Andrew speak:

Every believer *has* the Holy Spirit dwelling in him; he ought to know this, and believe that the Spirit will work in him what he needs for further growth and strength. The difference arises when the question comes to the *way* in which the

believer is to *attain* the full experience of all that
the indwelling of the Spirit implies.

Two answers have been set forth: Believe that
He is within you, open up and surrender your
whole being to Him and He will fill you; and the
second, Wait before God for this filling as a
special distinct gift, the fulfillment of the
Father's promise. I do not believe that the Word
of God teaches that *every* believer must
consciously seek and receive, as a *distinct
experience*, such a baptism. But I believe that it
is in harmony with the teaching of Scripture that
in answer to believing prayer, many believers
have received, and those who seek it *will often
receive*, such an inflow of the Spirit of God as
will to them indeed be nothing less than a *new*
baptism of the Spirit.

Let us not fall into the extreme of saying that,
since God has given and we have received the
Spirit, we are no longer to *pray for more* of Him.
It is often questioned, But how can you ask for
that which you already have? Our lungs are full
of breath, and yet call for a fresh supply every
moment; our fingers pulse with the fullness of
blood, yet continually call to the heart for a fresh
supply. . . . So our whole life of prayer should be
the harmony of faith that praises for the Spirit
that has been received, and yet always waits for
His fuller inflow out of Him in whom all fullness
dwells. . . . It would indeed be sad if a believer, on
once having received the Spirit, were to feel that
the "how much more" of Jesus' promise was
something he had now outgrown, and that this

chief of blessings he need no longer ask for. No! As the anointing with fresh oil is a daily need, just so the thought of Jesus baptizing with the Spirit is not a remembrance of what is a *past* thing, done once for all, but a promise of what may and should be a daily, continuous experience. The faith that we have the Spirit within us, even when it has almost come like a new revelation, and filled us with joy and strength, *will lose* its freshness and its power *except* as the inflow is *maintained* in living fellowship with the Father and the Son.

Andrew summarized his own teachings in the following distilled statements:

To the disciples, the baptism of the Spirit was very distinctly *not* His first bestowal for regeneration, but the definite communication of the presence in *power* of their glorified Lord.

Of this Spirit, *every* believer is made a partaker; he *has* the Spirit of Christ dwelling in him.

There may be, and in the great majority of Christians is, a contrast in their experience before and after the filling of the Spirit, just as was the state of the disciples before and after Pentecost. This difference, between the bare knowledge of His presence and the full revelation of the indwelling Christ in His glory, is due either to ignorance or unfaithfulness.

When once the distinct recognition of what the indwelling of the Spirit was meant to *bring* is realized by the believer, and he is ready to give up all to partake of it, he may ask and expect what may be termed a baptism of the Spirit. He may receive such an inflow of the Holy Spirit as shall consciously lift him to a different level from the one on which he has hitherto lived.

The *way* in which the baptism comes may be very different. To some it comes as a glad and sensible quickening of their spiritual life. They are so filled with the Spirit that all their *feelings* are stirred. They can speak of something they have distinctly *experienced* as a gift from the Father.

To others it is given, not to their feelings, but to their *faith*. It comes as a deep, quiet, but clearer insight into the fullness of the Spirit in Christ as indeed being theirs, and a faith that feels confident that His sufficiency is equal to every emergency that may arise. In the midst of weakness they know that the Power is resting on them. *In either case* they know that the blessing *has been given from above*, to be maintained in obedience and deep dependence on Him from whom it came.

Such a baptism is specially given as *power for work*. It may sometimes be received before the believer fully understands his calling to a ministry for others, and while he is chiefly occupied with his own sanctification. But it cannot be maintained except as the call to *witness for the Lord* is obeyed. The baptism at Pentecost and thereafter was distinctly given as preparation for witness. We must beware of laying down fixed rules [as to the manifestations of that baptism]. God's gifts and love are larger than our hearts. Every believer who longs, up to the light that he has, to be fully surrendered to the glory of his Lord, may come and claim the fullness of the gift. It will prove its own power to *open the mouth* and bring forth testimony for God.... To some people, the fullness of the Holy Spirit may come without any idea of a baptism at all; in intense devotion to their Lord, they *know* that He dwells in them, and has them *wholly* as His own.

Andrew taught that the natural temperament of a person had something to do with the kind of response he or she has to the baptism or filling of the Holy Spirit; also that the Holy Spirit sovereignly comes upon individuals and groups of believers in *different ways* at *different times.* Those who received it variously are not to criticize those who differ, or discount their experiences as being unbiblical or invalid. He illustrated it beautifully from the South African scene with which he was most familiar:

In our country, where we often suffer from drought, we find two sorts of reservoirs for catching and storing water. On some farms you have a spring or well but with a stream too weak to irrigate with. There a reservoir is made for collecting the water, and the filling of the reservoir is the result of the gentle, quiet inflow from the fountain day and night.

In other cases, the farm has no spring; the reservoir is built in the bed of a stream or in a hollow where, when rain falls, the water can be collected. In such a place, the filling of the reservoir, with a heavy fall of rain, is often the sudden work of a very few hours, and is accompanied with a rush and violence not free from danger. The noiseless supply of the former farm is the surer, because the supply, though apparently weaker, is permanent.

There is the same difference in the way in which the fullness or baptism of the Spirit comes and also the response to it. On the day of Pentecost, or at times when new beginnings are made, or in the outpouring of the Spirit of conversion in heathen lands, or of revival among Christian people, suddenly, mightily, manifestly, men are filled with the Holy Ghost. In the enthusiasm and the joy of the newly found salvation or revival, the power of the Spirit *is undeniably* present.

And yet, for those who receive it thus, there are special dangers. The blessing is often too much dependent on the fellowship with others, or extends only to the upper and more easily reached currents of the soul's life; the sudden is often, though not always, the superficial; the depths of the will and the inner life sometimes have not been reached.

There are other Christians who have never been partakers of any such marked experience, and in whom, nevertheless, the fullness of the Spirit is no less distinctly seen in the deep and intense devotion to Jesus, in a walk in the light of His countenance and the consciousness of His holy presence, in the blamelessness of a life of simple trust and obedience, and in the humility of a self-sacrificing love to all around.

And which of these is now the *true* way of being filled or baptized with the Spirit? The answer is easy. There are farms on which both the above-named reservoirs are to be found, auxiliary to each other. There are even reservoirs in which both the modes of filling are made use of. The regular, quiet, daily inflowing keeps them supplied in time of great drought; in time of rain they are ready to receive and store up large supplies.

There are some Christians who are not content unless they have special mighty visitations of the Spirit: the rushing mighty wind, floods outpoured, and the baptism of fire — these are their symbols.

There are others to whom the fountain springing up from within, and quietly streaming forth, appears the true type of the Spirit's work.

Happy are they who can *recognize God in both,* and hold themselves always ready to be blessed *in whichever way He comes!*

With such beautifully balanced Scriptural insights, it is no wonder that Andrew Murray spans the generations as a "mountaineer of the higher life"!

21

Missionary Statesman

Andrew Murray is best known for his ministry of the deeper life and the edification of believers, themes reflected in many of his writings. But he had a heart for missions which was hardly equaled by any of the missionaries of his day or ours. From his childhood contacts with missionaries in the Graaff-Reinet parsonage, and his firsthand opportunities to hear the great missionaries of his day while studying in Scotland and Holland as a young man, his passion had been to reach all people for Christ — in his own country of Africa and wherever the waves washed on distant shores. He and his brother John had even been instrumental in establishing a student missionary group in Holland while in divinity school.

When Andrew began his ministry in South Africa in 1848, the modern missionary era was only half a century old. Up to that point, about a dozen or so missionary societies had begun work at the Cape.

Andrew's missionary vision always lay close to the surface of his call from God, and he sought every opportunity to fan it into flames in the church. At a meeting of the synod in Cape Town in 1857 some far-reaching decisions were made, among them that a forward step should be taken in regard to mission work. A missionary committee had already been appointed, but its senior members were cautious and not very enthusiastic. They argued that their burden for the scattered *white* population in South Africa was already a heavy one and ministers were scarce anyway — one third of the churches were without pastors. How could there be thought of outreach to others?

The younger men, including the Murrays, had come in touch with the missionary work of the ministers in Scotland and had learned what God was doing in other countries as well as having come into direct contact with thousands of tribal people in the Free State and Transvaal. They wanted to move forward. A new committee was formed which represented the dawn of a new era in the Dutch Reformed Church and the beginning of its now widespread and successful missionary work.

For half a century Andrew continued to guide the mission policy of the Dutch Reformed Church. During the thirty years between 1886 and 1916, out of a total of some seventy who enlisted in the foreign missions program of the church, no less than twenty-one young men, who were sons of ministers and missionaries entered the foreign mission field, and of this number fifteen belonged to the *Murray* family! Of Andrew's own children, his second daughter, Mary, and his sons John and Charles gave themselves to mission work.

As a result of the Worcester conference, and the revival that followed, the missions impetus greatly increased, and this despite the fact that the Dutch

Church in South Africa at that time numbered only
fifty-three ministers. One of their initial burdens was
for the tribal people of the Transvaal. Two of the
ministers who had been recruited from Europe, as has
been mentioned, came for missionary work. Andrew
was asked to accompany them to the North and help
make arrangements for the starting of the work. They
were to be the first foreign missionaries of the Dutch
Reformed Church to go beyond the boundary of the
Colony and were the fruit of many prayers.

The journey was to be about a thousand miles, a
difficult and time-consuming trip. Reaching Pretoria,
Andrew had to confer with the members of the
Executive Council resident at the capital. They were
granted permission to begin missionary work, but only
on one condition — that the consent of the tribal chief
of the given district be secured beforehand. They had
not considered that this would be a problem, but were
stopped short by a resounding "No!" from a large
gathering of some forty petty chiefs who were asked
whether they would have a teacher.

The missionaries were deeply tried and troubled by
this setback and waited and prayed for a meeting with a
second group of twelve chiefs. Again they received a
rebuff. Andrew ultimately had to return to Worcester,
leaving the potential missionaries behind in language
study, patiently waiting in quiet faith until it should
please God to open the door — which was not until two
years later.

Andrew wrote to his wife concerning the episode:
". . . It was during these days of waiting that the thought
of the blessing of the indwelling Spirit appeared so clear
to me, the prospect of being filled with Him, at
moments so near that I could almost feel sure we would

yet attain this happiness. The wretchedness of the uncertain life we mostly led, the certainty that it cannot be the Lord's pleasure to withhold from His bride the full communion of His love, the glorious prospect of what we could be and do if *truly filled* with the Spirit of God — all this combines to force one to be bold with God and say, 'I will not let Thee go except Thou bless me.' "

It appears that there was a deeper, more lasting experience of the fullness of the Holy Spirit that Andrew had not yet settled into. There was still a longing for more of God's richness.

He continued to write to his wife: "Yesterday I preached from the words 'Be filled with the Spirit,' and am only strengthened in the conviction that it is our calling just to take God's Word, setting forth what we are to be, as it stands, and seek and expect it, even though we cannot exactly comprehend what it means. In all the experience of the blessings of the gospel, the intellect must follow the heart and the life.

"We did not forget on Saturday evening that it was, if I calculate aright, the anniversary of the beginning of the great revival movement. May the Lord now grant us His Spirit, that all who believe may be filled with His grace and become entirely His."

Having to return without a mission accomplished, in the sense that they had hoped to establish foreign mission work immediately, was not a discouraging defeat to Andrew. He was learning many difficult but precious lessons of waiting, which eventually became the basis of his book *Waiting on God*. He wrote at that time, "I feel a quiet but strong confidence that the work is the Lord's and that, if I may say it, the responsibility of it is His."

Andrew's books were thus written in response to freshly personal and local needs, and in so doing he began to reach out to an ever enlarging circle of readers who identified with those needs.

In appealing to the churches on behalf of missions, Andrew wrote in a tract: "The Mission Committee has long spoken of extending the foreign missions work, but talking alone does not help; there are no laborers, and the work has been carried on for years with only three workers. Young men are not coming to be trained for the work. Thus it goes on year after year, and the heathen among whom we ought to labor are left in their darkness. The harvest is great and the laborers are few. The harvest is lost in the fields — Satan has no lack of men for saloon keepers — but the Lord Jesus seems to call in vain for missionaries!"

To meet the challenge he had just pointed out, when Andrew accepted the Wellington pastorate he turned his hand to a closely related project — the establishment in 1877 of a boys' boarding home where missionaries and teachers might be trained.

But he was learning never to initiate any ministry, no matter how worthwhile it seemed to him and to others, ". . . until quiet waiting upon God gave me the confidence to step out in faith on this new venture. . . . I feel that I have but one lesson to learn better and I am learning it: just to sit and adore and say to Divine Grace, that there is nothing I cannot expect His wondrous kindness to do."

He looked again to America for teachers, and was successful in starting the work with ten boarders. It developed into the Missionary Training Institute which, as the years went by, provided 145 ordained missionaries out of the 178 who were working in connection with the Dutch Reformed Church at a certain time. In 1905 this Institute passed into the hands of the Synod of the Dutch Reformed Church which carried it forward.

The uniqueness of the principles of this missionary institute was that it was for young men who wanted to work for the Lord, but who had no time, aptitude, or strong desire to pay much attention to intensive study of ancient languages or mathematics. The aim was to provide thorough Biblical and general training so that graduates could take their places in the church and in society both honorably and profitably. It offered to men who were no longer in their early youth the chance of obtaining a good general education through the medium of both English and Dutch, and to do so at minimum cost and adequate standard. It was, in essence, a Bible training school, rather than a seminary.

Andrew was always eager to encourage other Christian ministries, evangelistic services, missionary projects and specific works which the Lord had laid on the hearts of friends or strangers, whether they had any connection with his own church or not. To see the work of God's Kingdom go forward gave him the highest joy, and there was not a partisan feeling in his large heart. Whenever he would hear of another young man's burden for some new outreach for the gospel, he would immediately pray with the brother and seek the Lord with him, and give him all the support that could be mustered from every direction. This was especially true of any Christian or group that was kindled for missions. Andrew was eager to help them launch their undertaking.

No estimate of Andrew's influence as a leader of missionary thought and enterprise would be complete that did not take into account his intimate connection with the South Africa General Mission.* His interest dated from the time he met the twenty-three-year-old Spencer Walton at Keswick in England. The youth felt burdened for mission work in South Africa and Andrew gave him every encouragement. Eventually Walton came to Cape Town to hold meetings, with remarkable spiritual results, and the whole city was greatly stirred. Christians of every denomination were strengthened in their faith and stimulated to a life of greater consecration to Christ and to the service of their fellow men.

The Cape General Mission was established in 1889, with Andrew as president and Spencer Walton as director. From evangelism first among the white population who were leading irreligious and ungodly lives — primarily those who were beyond the reach of ordinary church effort — the mission quickly expanded to direct mission work among the tribal people in the fields unentered or insufficiently occupied. Swaziland, one of the neediest of South African fields, was soon entered, and later other districts. In time The Cape General Mission absorbed the South-East Africa Evangelistic Mission and emerged as the South Africa General Mission, with which Andrew continued to be deeply involved to the end of his life.

Mr. Walton and Andrew were also intrumental in inaugurating the annual convention at Wellington which became known as the South African Keswick.

When the general mission committee of the Cape church faced a serious deficit in 1908, Whitsunday (June

*Known today as the Africa Evangelical Fellowship.

7) was proclaimed a day of prayer. In Wellington, Andrew, who was by then retired, delivered a powerful sermon on the text, "Speak unto the children of Israel that *they go forward*" (Exodus 14:15). Those who heard it could never forget it. Three days later the consistory decided to convene a conference on this matter in August; on that occasion the Laymen's Mission League was founded and £700 was pledged. And after another series of mission conferences in which Andrew was involved, £10,000 was collected. Andrew inspired the movement and was the only one to attend all the conferences.

In his book *The Kingdom of God in South Africa* (1906) Andrew stated, "Prayer is the life of missions. Continual and believing prayer is the secret of the life-giving power and fruitfulness of mission work. The God of missions is the God of prayer."

22

Power for Outreach

The *South African Dictionary of National Biography* states:

It is difficult to select a *magnum opus* from the list of Murray's publications. Perhaps it is because his works were so profoundly spiritual and therefore qualitatively equal. Yet his two major mission works, *The Key to the Missionary Problem* (1901) and *The State of the Church* (1911), with their Dutch translations, are conspicuous because they are by no means ordinary publications; they are events in the history of the Christian Church. Both works represented Murray's reaction to world missionary conferences: the Ecumenical Missionary Conference in New York in 1900 and the World Missionary Conference in Edinburgh in 1910. Both proved that he had a knack, more so than any other writer, to place his finger on the salient point or final issue, and bring it to the notice of the world.

As an example of Andrew's impact upon his generation for the cause of missions, we will look more closely at the circumstances surrounding the writing of his most significant book on missions, *The Key to the Missionary Problem.*

"Andrew, what's in the telegram? The messenger boy said it was from New York."

Emerging from a baking task in the kitchen, wiping floured hands on her apron, Andrew Murray's wife, Emma, sat down on the veranda beside him. The year was 1899 and it was a special excitement to receive telegrams after having waited for months in previous years for letters to arrive by boat.

"It's an invitation to attend a missionary conference in New York next April, my dear. It will be the largest and most important ever held. They want me to speak."

"How can you go, Andrew?" Emma gazed thoughtfully and anxiously over the lawn and fields surrounding their home in Wellington, South Africa. She knew her husband's thoughts would also be upon the Anglo-Boer War which had just broken out and in which so many of their fellow Christians and even family members were involved.

"No, I believe it would not be God's will for me to leave my people at this critical time. I am needed here now to pray and preach and give what counsel I can toward stopping this dreadful bloodshed among brethren." His face, lined with the spiritual concerns of fifty years of shepherding his people, nevertheless reflected a peace that could only be divinely derived.

"You know how I feel about missions. I would so much like to be there. I will send them a telegram right away with my regrets and assure them of my prayers."

But the conference committee would not accept his refusal that easily because of his reputation and stature in the cause of missions. They followed with another more urgent invitation and a copy of the volume of agenda that had been issued in preparation for the conference, so that he might look it over.

Andrew searched his heart to be sure he understood God's leading not to go. "Do I have a message from the Lord for that meeting? Would I be able to give that message so clearly as to make it worthwhile to go all that distance? Would it be possible amid the great variety of subjects to secure quiet, time, and undivided attention for that which appears to me the one thing needful?"

The committee continued to approach him, this time through his friend Mr. D. L. Moody, pressing him to come, and after the conference inviting him to stay over and participate in Moody's meetings in Northfield. But Andrew still felt he should not attend. All the while, the topics on the agenda and the great missionary issues involved were burning in his heart.

"My mind became clearer," he wrote, "and I felt that the one point on which I would have wished to speak was this: How the Church could be roused to know and do our Lord's will for the salvation of men." The omission of very important spiritual considerations in that preliminary report bothered Andrew.

"I had received the impression that while very naturally the chief attention was directed to the work in the field, the work at home and the fitting of the Church for doing its part faithfully hardly had a place. I felt that the basic issue was: There is no more spiritual and mysterious truth than that Christ our Head is actually and entirely dependent upon the members of His body for carrying out the plans which He, as Head, has formed. It is only spiritual men, and a Church in which spiritual men have influence, that is capable of rightly carrying out Christ's commands. The clearest arguments, the most forcible appeals, avail little where this is not understood and aimed at as the true standard of Christian devotion."

Andrew felt very deeply that no question was more urgent than: How is the Church to be reached and led to place herself, with every member and with all her powers, at her Lord's disposal for the work for which He has destined her and depends on her?

Not only had the preliminary report hardly alluded to any such point, but after the conference, when he received the two volumes of the proceedings, he spent eager hours going over every message, report, resolution and quotation to see if such foundation truths had been dealt with. While indirectly and implicitly it was admitted that there was something wrong with the greater part of professing Christians that affected the missionary task, the real seriousness and sinfulness of the situation was *not* dealt with nor recommendations forthcoming as to what the churches and missionary societies could do to effect a change. Though acknowledging the many good things that came out of this landmark Ecumenical Missionary Conference, Andrew Murray felt that the lack was so strategic that he should write a small book to that point, *The Key to the Missionary Problem.*

In its first chapter he prefaced his forthcoming weighty and sober words with:

I know it is no easy task to humbly, wisely, lovingly and yet faithfully and effectually speak

of what appears lacking or sinful in the Church.
And yet I am sure that there are many who would
welcome help in answering the question: Is there
any prospect, any real possibility of such a
revival in the Church that proof will be given
that, as a whole, and in every congregation where
the full gospel is preached, her only aim will be
to carry the gospel to every creature? And if so,
what is the path that will lead to this great
change and what are the steps to be taken by
those who lead the missions of the Church?

That little volume exploded upon the churches in
America, Europe and South Africa in a way that perhaps
a spoken message on the occasion of the conference,
even by Andrew Murray, could never have done. As a
result we have in some more permanent form a
summons to action for missions as burning and
contemporary as it was almost fourscore years ago. It
was a book of great intensity which sounded forth a
rousing and solemn call to new activity, fresh
consecration, and more abundant prayer for the cause
of missions.

The four principles on which he based the book
were: that missions are the chief end of the Church; that
the chief end of the ministry is to guide the Church in
this work and fit her for it; that the chief end of
preaching ought to be to train the congregation to take
its part in helping the Church to fulfill her destiny; and
that the chief end of every minister in this connection
ought to be to seek grace to fit himself thoroughly for
this work.

The keynote of this volume is: The missionary
problem is a personal one; every believer is a soul-

winner; every minister holds office under the Great Commission; the missionary enterprise is the work not merely of all, but of each.

After dealing intelligently, knowledgeably, and deeply spiritually with important issues set in historical perspective and in the context of the Church worldwide, Andrew concluded the little volume with these burning words:

> Extraordinary circumstances require extraordinary measures. The discovery of an imminent danger justifies exceptional changes, and men willingly approve and submit to the inconvenience. The state of the Church, the need of the world, the command of Christ, appear to me to call for very special efforts. The urgency of the case is extreme. There is no time to be lost. Our Master wishes every human being without delay to know of His having come to the world to save him.
>
> Let not the enthusiasm of our watchword, IN THIS GENERATION! deceive us. It may make us content that meantime the millions a year who are passing away in darkness should not know Him. It may deceive us with the idea that it is certainly going to be done. But it is most certainly *not* going to be done if the Church remains at her present level.
>
> The one deep impression the Report of the Conference leaves is that, unless pastors and members labor and pray with an entirely new devotion, the work cannot possibly be accomplished. It is so large, it is so difficult, it

needs such an interposition of divine power, that, *unless the Church returns to the pentecostal life of her first love,* it cannot and will not be done!

I say again, the urgency of the case is extreme. No sacrifice can be too great if we can only get the Church, or the most earnest part of it, to take time and wait unitedly before the Throne of God, to review her position, to confess her shortcomings, to claim God's promise of power and to consecrate her all to His service.

The Key to the Missionary Problem produced an immediate and sober impression among church and mission leaders throughout the Christian world and spread like wildfire through the ranks of the laymen.

Dr. Handley Moule, Bishop of Durham, England, wrote of it: "With all my heart I recommend this volume to the perusal, the thought and the prayers of all ministers of Christ and His flock. It is an appeal to the inmost soul of the pastor, and at the same time a suggestion for the most practical possible application of his activities. The great Christian who writes it puts his main propositions with an urgency which, just here and there, as it seems to me, invites the recollection of other sides of truth. His contention that the missionary enterprise of the Church is its supreme call seems, in places, to become the assertion that it is its *one* real call. But no deep-sighted reader will really mistake these places. And every reader who has indeed set his eyes toward the will of God will rise from the perusal, or rather kneel down after it, asking, 'Lord, what wouldst Thou have *me* to do?' "

Dr. R. F. Horton, of Hampstead, said: "Six weeks ago I brought Andrew Murray's book before my church and they have bought and read about a hundred copies. I fervently trust that every *minister* will read it, for he makes clear that the key to the missionary problem is in the hand of the ministers: they open and no man can shut; they keep shut and no man can open. But I want the *people* to read it too, because it seems to me the most inspiring and inspired book written in 1901 — the true note of a new century."

With the same enthusiasm wrote Dr. Alexander Maclaren: "I hope that Mr. Murray's heart-searching book may be widely read and prayerfully pondered. It is *'The Key to the Missionary Problem'* indeed, but is it also the key to most of our problems and points to the only cure for all our weaknesses."

And Dr. F. B. Meyer added his testimony in the following terms: "Of all the books that I have *ever* read on the call of our Lord to the evangelization of the world, this appeal by the beloved Andrew Murray must stand in the front rank, if not first. My heart has been deeply moved by it, and I propose to read large portions of it to my people. If it were only read universally throughout our churches, by ministers and people alike, I believe it would lead to one of the greatest revivals of missionary enthusiasm that the world has ever known!"

An anonymous letter in Dutch in the foremost Christian magazine of that day in South Africa echoed these impressions: "Next to the man who *writes* me a good book, I place the man who *recommends* me a good book. A booklet came into my hands recently entitled *The Key to the Missionary Problem*. The writer is the

the well-known minister of Wellington. When I had read it, I thanked the Lord for it, though it condemned me grievously. I also prayed that the Lord would direct its distribution and make its perusal a blessing to thousands. It will yield matter for addresses at missionary prayer meetings much more glowing than those of last month and the month before. Nor is it a book for the minister only but for all who take even a slight interest in the advancement of God's Kingdom. I know of no better means of kindling increased interest in the extension of that Kingdom than the circulation of this work. Followers of Jesus who read it and do not thereafter pray in a different manner to what they did before, must have a different spiritual constitution from that of the writer of these lines."

At the conclusion of his book, Andrew proposed that the subjects for the up-coming week of prayer, to be chosen by the Council of the Evangelical Alliance for January, 1902, should deal exclusively with the relation of the Church to the Great Commission. Many regretted that this was not carried out, but was modified to suggest that Christians should set aside a portion of time each day for the purpose of special intercession on behalf of missions.

Had Andrew's suggestion been followed, the writer of one of his biographies felt that there could be no doubt that a wonderful increase of missionary fervor thoughout Christendom would have been the result. As it was, his proposal was adopted and carried out only in South Africa.

But there the results were very striking. In the course of 1902 the Boer War ended. With the proclamation of peace, Boer prisoners began to return from the various military camps in which they had been incarcerated in India and Ceylon, on St. Helena and on Bermuda. It turned out that more than one hundred and fifty young men who had accepted Christ as their Lord and Master in the camps now volunteered to go forth, after the necessary training, and *become missionaries among the peoples of Africa.* A special institution was founded in 1903 for this purpose and the Boer Missionary Institute at Worcester may be regarded as an indirect result of the concentrated prayer to which the Dutch Reformed Church was roused through the influence of this book, *The Key to the Missionary Problem.*

A reader of this book from Somersetshire just after its issue wrote, "I have been greatly profited by reading your book on missions. I cannot help thinking that some effort should be made to bring it to the notice of every member of the various churches. I respectfully suggest the issue of a million copies (to start with) at one penny each!"

23

An Anointed Pen

Andrew Murray had to write. His spirit was too vast for the spoken word alone.

"Andrew, did you start out to be a popular writer?" we might ask him.

Surely he would laugh, with his easy sense of humor, and reply, "Certainly not, nor would I ever have believed that anyone beyond my rustic parish would be interested in my writing. But the Lord's hand became most evident upon it." Then, with a twinkle in his eye, "And Emma's hand, too."

His early writing was designed as a simple help to the mothers of his flock, who, with their large families averaging a dozen or more children, had the main duty to teach the first principles of Christianity to their children along with basic reading and writing skills. Most of his wilderness congregation in the early years of his pastorate were scattered on lonely farms fifty or a hundred miles from Bloemfontein and rarely able to get to church.

"What was your first book, Andrew, and how did you feel about it?"

"My writing debut was in 1858 with a Life of Christ in the language of children which I had published in Europe. When I held the first precious copy in my hands, I exclaimed, 'I like it, but am disappointed that it is not more simple. There are passages that I hardly believe I myself have written!' "

Jesus, the Children's Friend, written originally in Dutch, was never translated into English because there were so many other good books of that nature in English. About this book Andrew commented to his brother John, "I was glad to see the advertisement of it. I would only wish my name left out of it. What do you think, from your experience, will be the time needed to get in the capital that has been laid out? You have never yet let me know what the printer's bill comes to. I would be sorry if you should suffer the least inconvenience in making my money arrangements. . . . Let me know, too, what impression the thing makes."

It may seem strange that such a serious man like Andrew launched his writing career in the field of children's books. But all of his life he had a beautiful rapport with children and youth; they took an immediate liking to him, feeling at home in his presence. His children's sermons were always popular. When away from home preaching in the early years, he would gather children around him at any opportunity and tell them a story or hear them recite their texts and hymns — and give them some to be learned for next time. Even at the age of eighty-six, he held the rapt attention of a congregation of some 300 young people who listened to his explanation of the way of salvation — and at the close of a three-day retreat it was touching to see over a hundred profess Christ.

"My second book likewise related to children, but it was for parents," Andrew explains. "It was titled *What Manner of Child Shall This Be?* The contents were mainly meditations and baptismal addresses for believing parents which I delivered during my early country travels when on some occasions I had to baptize forty or fifty children each Sunday. I tried to be careful not to do it en masse, but to give individual instruction to parents, even if the rite was administered in a tent, a tiny room, or farmhouse. This book was designed to be a guide for them after I left." Later this book was published in English under the title *How to Raise Your Children for Christ.*

When he was already in his eighties, after retirement from his active pastorate, Andrew devoted even more time to the continuous writing of books and pamphlets. Whenever he would read something that would stimulate his mind or spirit, he reached for his pen to see what the Lord would speak to him on some new aspect of divine truth from that spark.

In his earlier years his wife took his dictation and was an eager sounding board for his ideas. His youngest daughter, Annie, acted as his actual writer during the latter years of his life because his own strength for direct writing with a pen was limited from an early illness. He would dictate for hours as Annie joyfully and patiently transcribed his thoughts.

One Good Friday morning, as they returned from church, Andrew had some fresh thoughts which wouldn't wait even until afternoon. "I must begin a new book right away," he said, and Annie was pressed into immediately taking down the titles of twenty chapters for a booklet on love.

Andrew's methods of writing were varied. Let's ask him about them.

"Which comes first, your titles or the chapter contents?"

"Sometimes the one, and sometimes the other," he confides. "But usually the outline is quite clear in my head first, and then I can fill things out as the Lord reveals further thoughts to me."

"Do you set aside certain times of the day for writing?" we ask, in pursuit of some insight into his method of producing such a quantity of manuscripts.

"Sometimes I get home from conferences and meetings of considerable strain and weariness," (we don't wonder, because you are in your eighties, Andrew!) "but I must still hurry to write before the ideas flee. The other day I had to apologize to Annie that we had to write without her getting any rest. We did two chapters and eight chapter headings within a few hours.

"And then sometimes I don't sleep so well. The other night, during the hours before dawn, I composed three chapters of a little volume that I will call *Christ Our Life*."

"Do you have an urge to write on certain topics, Andrew?"

"Well, I sometimes put it this way," he replies with a chuckle, "I am like a hen about to lay an egg. I am restless and unhappy until I get the burden of the message off my mind. And when a book is finished, I like to have it quickly forwarded to the printer. But not before Annie and I pause and render unto the Lord a humble word of thanksgiving for His gracious guidance in the writing."

"Would you share with us what you pray?"

"Lord, we have been endeavoring to instruct others; may we ourselves learn the truths Thou seekest to impart; and do Thou richly bless this book to all its readers. Amen."

Yes, Andrew, your prayers are being answered more abundantly than you ever could have imagined. The glory belongs to the Lord, as you have wanted it.

"And where did you get the idea for those handy vest-pocket booklets? Or were they an invention of some publisher?"

"My nephew, Rev. A. A. Louw, visited me one day late in 1912 and drew from his pocket a tiny booklet written by someone else. I thought, how convenient for believers always to have such little books to carry about and read at odd moments — on the cart, in the train, at the railway station, anywhere and everywhere — and to give to others at little cost. I let no time elapse before I composed the first of such a series of my own works, which was *Lord, Teach Us To Pray.*" (This book was later titled *The Secret of Intercession.*)

Twelve of these booklets came from Andrew's pen during the next five years, becoming the "Pocket Companion" series in English. Brief and to the point, these rich little booklets contain the cream of Andrew's teachings, written out of the ripe fullness of his experience in Christ.

"What would you say are the characteristics of your style, Andrew?"

"That is an unimportant subject to me," admits Andrew, "but apparently it interests others a great deal. I admire beauty and style in other writings, but I am very little concerned with my own. I lament that I have a miserable deficiency in composition. I have often said to Annie, 'My child, I have no style, or only a very bad style.' I have a burden on my heart from the Lord for that which I write, and I feel an urgency to deliver it and fulfill my solemn trust. Actually the form which that message assumes is not that vital a concern with me. When I was young and studying in Holland, I heard and read too much useless rhetoric from the pulpit and pen which was nothing but husks and stones without benefit to people. I want most of all to *feed* my people; the dish and tableware are not the direct means of nourishment!

"Many of my dear friends, however," he teases, "try to defend my style, or lack of it, by saying that I have bad English because I write in Dutch, and that I have bad Dutch because I think in English! Never mind; if God receives the glory and the sheep are fed, I am happy."

But thousands the world over appreciate and admire Andrew Murray's style, the strength and eloquence which is born of deep earnestness and solemn issues which stir hearts and minds to spiritual heights and depths. The writings of Andrew are described as "moving the emotions, searching the conscience, and winnowing sins and shortcomings."

Let us ask Annie about her father's writing habits, eager as we are to glean every detail.

"Father sits up very straight in his study chair and dictates to me in a loud, clear voice, as though he were actually addressing his audience. His hours of work are usually from nine to eleven in the forenoon, during which two or three chapters of a book may be completed."

"How about the punctuation and grammar and general format, Annie? Is that up to you?"

"Oh, Father is *very* particular about punctuation. And he always says, 'New paragraph,' pointing with his long, slender finger to the exact spot on my paper where the new line must begin. He says 'full-stop, comma, colon, semicolon' right where the sense would require. Should I make some mistake or spell something wrong, Father makes some playful remark like: 'You will have to go back to kindergarten, you know!'

"At eleven o'clock he says (when I myself am quite tired!), 'Now give me ten minutes rest — or no, let us write some letters for a change.' Then half a dozen letters are quickly dictated, in reply to requests for prayer for healing, for the conversion of relatives, for the deliverance of friends addicted to drink; or they might be business letters. Occasionally he dictates letters for Christian magazines on the state of the Church, or for the newspaper on some matters affecting the country.

"Father always tucks the manuscript of a new book inside the pages of some magazine or journal for safekeeping. Then he will say, 'Now bring me *Father Christmas*,' and the manuscript pages of one of the "Pocket Companion" series is produced from within its covers, which had shielded it from being scattered."

"Does your father stop writing when he is ill?"

"If at all able, he keeps writing. When recovering, he always writes in bed. Even when weak, he dictates in a tone of great earnestness. And he has fussy ideas of how much writing I should get on a page. 'Write closer, closer,' he often repeats. When near the final page, he will say, 'Now the last four lines for a prayer'; then he folds his hands, closes his eyes, and actually prays the prayer which ends the written meditation."

It is rather difficult to analyze the periods of Andrew's literary career too distinctly. He did pass through clearly defined stages of spiritual growth and these can be traced in his writings, though his early books show remarkable maturity of thought and experience. In fact, all the teachings of his lifetime were present in embryo in some of his first major works, and they came forth one by one in greater intensity and depth as the years went by and his experiences increased. This emphasis is noticeable in the way Andrew underscored, had italicized, or printed in bold type certain words and sentences which he considered important in his books.

His first writings might be said to emphasize the *edification* of believers — their building up in faith and love and prayer. To this class belong *Abide in Christ, Like Christ, The New Life,* and others.

After 1888 the subject of *sanctification* gripped him, of which *Holy in Christ* is an example.

The final period may be characterized as stressing *intercessory prayer,* launched with *The State of the Church* in 1911. Still, the dividing lines are only vague and the subjects overlap.

Andrew was not a mystic in the sense of one who ignores the problems and hurts of his times. As the prophets of old, he never failed to speak out with insight and authority at critical moments in the history of his country and the Church and the world. He raised his voice and his pen to direct attention to the real issues. He was said to "possess the gift of speaking at the right season, of having the right and just word, and of opening up the larger view and kindling the nobler emotions." This was echoed in his writings as he went beyond superficial symptoms to reach ultimate causes.

So universal were his teachings on the Christian faith that they leaped over ethnic and cultural barriers and were translated with equal profit into French, German, Italian, Spanish, Swedish, Danish, Russian, Yiddish, Arabic, Armenian, Telugu, Malaysian, Japanese and Chinese. A previous biographer stated, "Countless persons in every quarter of the globe hail Andrew Murray as their spiritual father, and ascribe whatever growth their Christian life has undergone to the influence of his priceless devotional works."

"Did you make money on your book sales, Andrew?"

"I was happy enough if I realized back the investment of publishing them! As for translations, my books frequently appeared in other languages even without my knowledge or my previous permission, so of course I got no financial profit from them; neither did I want it. Whenever I was asked permission to allow a book to be translated, I freely and gladly gave it."

"Do you know of specific instances in countries of totally different culture where your books have been a blessing in translation?"

"Oh, many letters come to me, some in foreign languages. For just one illustration, a missionary of the Christian Literature Society for China reported that when traveling in the interior of China, another missionary informed him of a striking discovery she had made. Apparently she had some of my books on her bookshelf but had not read them; one day she was led to do so and was filled with the Holy Spirit. The impact of that testimony led the journeying missionary to read my books also, and to translate *The Spirit of Christ* into Chinese. He informed me that it passed through many editions, and it was widely reported what spiritual good it had done among the Chinese Christians.

"He told me of one city where a revival broke out through that book in Chinese; in another case, a Chinese pastor preached on it Sunday by Sunday, a chapter a week as a subject, and the church was tremendously revived. The prayer cycle at the end of my book *The Ministry of Intercession* was translated into Chinese and adapted to the Chinese church. *With Christ, Abide in Christ*, and several of my other books have likewise blessed the Chinese church, for which I do praise God."

"Can you give us a particular instance when a certain piece of your writing arose from one of your life-situations and turned into a blessing for others?"

"There were many; almost all of my teachings and writings were motivated by experiences through which I passed. For a brief example then — when I visited England again in 1895, I had a recurrence of my back trouble resulting from the accident in Natal when I was thrown from a capsizing cart. I was to speak one evening at Exeter Hall and there was some doubt if I would be strong enough. Besides, through some misunderstandings of expressions I had used in a message, which had given offence to some and provoked hostile criticisms, I would also have been prone to be disturbed and distressed in mind. On top of that, when my hostess brought me breakfast, she informed me of a person who was seeking my counsel and was in great trouble.

" 'Well, just give her this paper which I have been writing for myself; it may be that she will find it helpful,' I said on that occasion. It happened that my little message of assurance to myself of God's

appointment in my time of adversity was so appr
by my friends that they had it printed on card
distributed in large quantities."

"Please do repeat it for us!"

"Very well:

IN TIME OF TROUBLE SAY:

First—
God brought me here; it is by His will I am in this strait place: in that I will rest.

Next—
He will keep me in His love, and give me grace in this trial to behave as His child.

Then—
He will make the trial a blessing, teaching me the lessons He intends me to learn, and working in me the grace He means to bestow.

Last—
In His good time He can bring me out again— how and when He knows.

Say: I am here—
1. By God's appointment.
2. In His keeping.
3. Under His training.
4. For His time.

Psalm 50:15"

"Usually writers are wide readers of other books. Are you? And which books or authors have significantly influenced your life?"

"In my student years, certainly I did much reading. And in my uncle's home in Scotland I was thrown into a great reading atmosphere because the manse was well supplied with church magazines, missionary periodicals, theological and devotional books, and works of general literature. Missionary biographies were my particular favorites. During the years of our marriage, Emma and I read together on a regular basis, or I asked her to read to me as I relaxed after meetings. She was a cultured and well-read lady from her youth and kept bringing the importance of reading before me, which delight we shared together in spite of the ceaseless activity of our growing and spirited family. I have always kept in touch through periodicals with what is going on in the Christian world at large, as well as the matters of the nations."

"Novels he will *not* read," adds Annie. "But biographies are Father's delight. His bookshelves are crowded with works in the educational as well as the religious field. Some of his favorites are those of Fox, Brainerd, Wesley, Burns, Bonar, Muller, Moody, and Hudson Taylor."

Never wanting to keep to himself his discoveries from the reading of good books, Andrew regularly would read aloud to his family at mealtimes the passages which had struck him as memorable. He had heard this done in his childhood home, again in his uncle's manse in Scotland, and perpetuated it in his own family circle with great profit to all. He had the habit of writing quotations and moral axioms on little cards for future use. One that was written on a shop ticket, taken from his dressing gown, was "Live in that which should be, and you will transform that which is."

"Andrew, you must have had some particular interest in William Law; you edited selections from several of his books. Who was he and why do you feel he was significant?"

"Law was born in 1686, an English clergyman who studied at and was a fellow at Cambridge. But owing to his refusal to take the oath of allegiance to George I, he lost his position there and was, in effect, blacklisted by the state church. The subsequent enforced inactivity proved to be the doorway into a life of meditation and prayer.

"Law's life was greatly influenced by the works of Jacob Boehme, who taught him that which he had only faintly seen before, that God not only *is all*, and must *have all*, but that He alone must *do all*. He wrote on the nature and practice of intimacy with God. The more I read of his writings, the more I am impressed by his insight, range, and power. To share Law's spiritual depths in a more readable way with other Christians, I have edited selections from some of his books."

"But Andrew, was not Law a controversial figure? Even evangelically unorthodox in very basic doctrines?"

"Law did, indeed, represent the mysticism of his period which carried with it certain non-evangelical conclusions. Both Jacob Boehme, who influenced the later years and philosophy of Law, and Law himself, were unorthodox in many of their tenets. I am aware of these problems and have written a clear word of explanation to the Christian public. But it is because I believe Law's teachings supply what many are looking for, that I venture to recommend them. I do so in the confidence that no one will think that I have done so because I consider the truths that he denies are matters of minor importance, or that I have any sympathy with his erroneous views. . . . It often happens that where one side of the truth has laid powerful hold, another aspect has been neglected or denied. This was markedly the case with William Law . . . . "

It is enough to say that Andrew Murray, while laying stress on the supreme and positive message of mysticism — the necessity for union with the Divine — avoided the errors to which it is prone. His training in evangelical and reformed theology was so thorough, and his study of Scripture so excellent and continuous, as to keep him from going astray into the byways of mystical speculation. Andrew's own intense interest in mysticism he ascribed mainly to J. T. Beck, the German theologian, but the medieval Jan van Ruusbroec, Madame Guyon, Count Zinzendorf and the other German Pietists also influenced him.

The three books that are presently in print of Murray's editing of William Law's works are *Wholly for God, Freedom From a Self-Centered Life,* and *The Power of the Spirit.* Andrew sought to help some readers who might not at once be able to take in Law's teachings firsthand, or have opportunity to study them thoroughly, to see what his main points were.

"Andrew, do you feel that you yourself must fully understand and live out every topic that you write about?"

"It often happens that after I have spoken in a conference or even after I have written a book, that it is only then I begin to see the importance and meaning of

the truth with which I have been occupied. Later, some
of the very vital truths that I have set forth come home
to my own heart with special power as I apply them to
new situations in my life or in the teaching of others."

"I remember," adds Annie, "when Father was
preparing for bed one night recently, I saw a copy of his
own book *The State of the Church* under his arm.
Drawing it out, he said, 'Many a minister or other friend
has said to me that he has read this book. Yes, they have
read it through and then put it on their study shelves
among other books they have completed. Now *I* have
written this book myself, and yet *I* have to read it and re-
read it, so that I may be able to take in the true state of
the Church and be suitably moved by it.' "

"Do you have some counsel, Andrew, for those who
read your books?"

"Yes, the disposition of mind is very important. My
books should not be read quickly or superficially or
only once. They are to be meditated upon to gain the
fullest nourishment. More than that, it is not enough
that the reader should understand and appropriate my
thoughts, and then rejoice because of some new insight
he has obtained — or stop with the pleasure which that
knowledge has brought. There is something else — he
must surrender himself to the truth so that he shall be
ready, with an undivided will, *immediately to perform
all* that he shall learn to be God's will.

"I would suggest that the reader verbalize it this way:
'What God says, I will do; and if I see that anything is
according to His will, I will immediately receive it and
act upon it.' "

"Annie, was there another particular book which
your father desired to write but never did?"

"Oh yes, one especially. He had been gathering resource books on the topic for many years, some of them in German. He earnestly hoped to write on the outpouring of the Holy Spirit upon the Moravians in 1727, and its relation to missions, in connection with the life of Count Zinzendorf. But he was not able to do so before the Lord promoted him to Glory."

Ripening Years — Climbing Higher

"What if we can't get along?" hesitatingly asked the appointee associate-pastor, Rev. J. R. Albertyn, before accepting a position as colleague of such a well-known minister as Andrew.

"Come along, my brother," replied Andrew. "I will agree with you; only be sure you are always in the right!"

The two became close friends in the Wellington pastorate and Andrew was freed for a great deal more travel for evangelistic services. The Murrays vacated the parsonage and built their own home on a most beautiful site nearby. They called it "Clairvaux" after the famous abbey which Bernard of Clairvaux founded on the plains of Champagne. It continued to be a hub of hospitality to all until the end of Andrew's life.

Mealtimes, especially, were times when all who lived under the Murray roof gathered not only for food for the body but for fellowship and spiritual sharing — from the oldest to the youngest. One guest commented, "Meals with the Murrays are like Holy Communion."

On the occasion of Andrew's seventieth birthday, 1898, his ministerial jubilee was also celebrated, and for almost a week there were celebrations in his church and in all the schools and missions with which he was involved. His old university in Aberdeen conferred on him the honorary degree of D.D. (Later, in 1907, he was awarded a D. Lit. from the University of the Cape of Good Hope.) In recognition of the 1000 teachers who had been sent out from the Huguenot Seminary which Andrew founded, £1000 was raised as a special birthday gift for Andrew for the school.

For nearly a quarter of a century, Andrew had been re-elected as moderator of his church, the highest office, for which he was uniquely gifted. He knew the strength and weakness of his church and had initiative and persistent energy enough to carry through his purposes. His business ability and insight into the basic truth of any matter, and his knowledge of church law, gave him almost unerring judgment. He knew human nature and how to intervene in a debate at the psychological moment, while his ready wit and humor often cleared a highly charged atmosphere of dangerous elements. He was firm without being obstinate, tolerant without being weak, impartial without being irresolute. He was courteous, tactful in public, and readily accessible in private.

Andrew was active in the Ministers Association, and even when well over seventy, rose to catch the 6:15 morning train to Cape Town for its monthly breakfast and conference. "The lesson I have learned after a half century of ministerial work is that God has for every man a sphere of work and a plan of work. The more unreservedly a man submits to God's will, the more completely God's work is carried out."

Emma did worry about him when he undertook strenuous trips in the Free State for evangelistic work and threw himself so energetically into it. She wrote to her family, "I fear sometimes that Andrew will be laid to rest in that country of his first love ... but I have ceased to be anxious about him and only trust. It is God who gives him strength and will give it as long as He sees best. But some have remarked that when he is gone, six ministers will not be able to do his work. He is just head over ears in *missions*, and what can be done to rouse the Church to its calling to live for the Kingdom of God."

In 1899 the Anglo-Boer war broke out and Andrew and his family suffered much heart anguish because of friends and relatives on both sides. Many of his old friends turned away from him, some criticizing that he was too pro-Boer and others that he was too pro-British. There were church leaders on both sides, but they would not heed Andrew's call to come together in prayer. Andrew reached out in spiritual concern to the prisoners of war in the camps, trying to find chaplains acceptable to both sides, and taking charge of many of the services himself. The Lord moved mightily among the men in these camps, and many were converted. One hundred and fifty of them actually entered missionary training institutions at the conclusion of the war.

The strain of the war affected Andrew keenly and his health deteriorated. With his wife and two daughters, he spent some time in Switzerland to recuperate and devote quiet time in prayer. After peace was declared, the Murrays returned home.

In 1905 Emma was suddenly promoted to Glory, apparently through a stroke. The severing of their happy union of nearly fifty years was a heavy blow to the

ew, though his immediate prayer of
to God after her passing lifted the family
of Heaven. He preached as usual the
following Sunday, on the text "With Christ, which is far
better." He threw himself into work for the Lord so
strenuously that he himself had a slight stroke which
kept him in bed for some weeks. This situation
precipitated his decision to retire from the
responsibility of being in charge of a congregation, and
so, after fifty-seven years in the ministry, he became
Pastor Emeritus, continuing to live at "Clairvaux."

But the Lord had a still wider ministry for His
servant for the remaining twelve years of his life; he
became closely involved in the "Keswick Convention"
ministries.

That which became known as "Keswick" teaching,
had, in fact, been a part of Andrew's inner experience
and spiritual life-style throughout most of his life.
Because it was said that Emma's spiritual life mirrored
that of her husband most beautifully, Emma's record of
the essence of that teaching is valuable:

"There is a step higher than just looking forward to
Heaven. We may have our life so in Christ that even here
below we may enjoy peace and happiness in Him which
no earthly events can shake or destroy. And it is not by
despising or trampling upon earthly things, but *living
above them*; willing and loving to live for His glory and
the good of others, and counting it all joy even in
tribulation, for His sake.

"God means us to know, and experience, that perfect
peace and quiet of mind under all circumstances *is
possible*. Nothing interferes more with work or renders
it more difficult than fretting or worrying. In such a

state of mind we can do nothing well. We must in a childlike way acknowledge God's will in everything, with His peace in our hearts, and a truly humble walk with God, a bowing to His will. . . .

"All this is attainable through the *indwelling of the Holy Spirit* of God, through receiving Christ as our Sanctification, as well as our Justification; through an entire, unconditional surrender of ourselves to Him, and an entire cessation from our own efforts and works, while waiting for the suggestions and influences of the Holy Spirit; through believing in His indwelling and expecting His guidance even in the minutest concerns of our daily life."

Andrew kept closely in touch with the great spiritual movements of the world through reading books by their leaders and listening to reports of friends who had been involved with conferences. The Holiness Movement had begun in America and England and many Christians were stirred to deeper spiritual lives. The writings of Dr. Boardman, Dr. Cullus, Hudson Taylor, and George Muller echoed in Andrew's spiritual life.

One of his biographers described his development: "A profound though quietly wrought change was taking place in Mr. Murray. A born ruler of men, he nevertheless sought and obtained from God, from this point forward, a remarkable measure of the meekness and gentleness of Christ. It was wonderful how these qualities, united with humility and patience, marked the following years without any loss of strength."

Andrew prayed from that time on "to be made a fountain of love to all around," and it was evident to all that this was indeed a mark of the Lord upon him. "It is no new Christ or Christology, but Christ in a new and nearer aspect. It is an open secret to those whom God teaches," Andrew explained.

In due time Andrew came to be recognized as one of the leading Holiness teachers of the world, and so invitations to minister in conferences were many. In 1895 he went to England at the invitation of the Keswick Convention. Situated in England's famous Lake District, this convention was known throughout the Christian world for its annual conferences to promote greater spiritual intensity. Andrew's addresses were full of power and fire, in spite of the fact that his physical appearance was worn and weak. "One feels the presence of Christ whenever with him," was the continuous comment.

Describing Andrew's effect upon the Keswick audiences, Rev. Evan H. Hopkins, father of the Keswick movement in England, related, "His addresses came home to so many with peculiar power... it seemed as if none could escape, as if none could choose but to let Christ Himself, in the power of His living Spirit, be the One to live, although the cost was our taking the place of death. . . . As Mr. Murray dwelt on this more and more deeply as the days went on, especially at the solemn evening meetings, there came over some of us a memory of the early days of Keswick when an awe of God fell upon the whole assembly in a way that the writer has never seen equaled. . . ."

Andrew went to America immediately after, to the Northfield Convention, at the urgent invitation of D. L. Moody. For two weeks Andrew conducted the morning sessions with one theme totally absorbing him: the feeble and sickly religious life of the Church. In addition to the general public, four hundred ministers, including Mr. Moody himself and Dr. A. T. Pierson, attended these meetings, and testified to great blessing from Andrew's preaching. Dr. Pierson joined Andrew in conventions at Toronto, Boston, Chicago, New York and elsewhere. He testified to taking a new step of consecration at Andrew's meetings, after which his deepened spiritual life led him to lay somewhat less emphasis on the work of foreign missions and more on the Spirit of Christ *in all* of life and service.

Andrew's observation from his North American travels was: "The spiritual life of the pulpit has not struck us so much as that of the home and the individual. As in England, the pulpit aims too much after literary culture and cannot get this without paying for it — a heavy price — the 'wisdom of words making the cross of none effect.' "

Crossing back over to Holland for a remarkable succession of meetings, Andrew addressed a crowd of over two thousand people from the very pulpit of the Cathedral at Utrecht before which, at his confirmation fifty years before, he had first made public profession of his faith in Christ. At more than half a dozen other Dutch cities, crowds flocked to his services and an awakening of deep spiritual dimensions ensued.

He moved on to Ireland and Scotland before returning to London for a large Spiritual Life Convention, where he made seven speeches within three days, delivering his discourses, as usual, without benefit of manuscript or notes. His specific message was, "How sooner and more completely we can not only believe in, but have a full realization of our completeness in Christ Jesus." And again, "You must learn to know and trust Omnipotence. Let us make God's omnipotence the measure of our *expectation*. . . . We must take God at His word and return to the rapture and fire of the first apostleship. .... God will put no difference between the Church of that time and ours in the results that He will give us to reap."

For the last twenty-eight years of his life, Andrew was considered the father of the Keswick movement in South Africa. Patterned along the lines of the English Keswick Convention, its teachings were generally along the line of whole-hearted consecration to God. Speakers proclaimed the possibility of a child of God being so filled with and led by the Holy Spirit that a life well-pleasing to God may be lived here on earth. Andrew became the president and chairman of the South African Keswick and continued as such until his death.

Basic topics of the Convention were: the necessity of entire surrender to the Lord; complete cleansing from sin through the precious Blood; and the fullness and anointing of the Holy Spirit for life and service. The results of the annual conferences were far reaching upon the Church of Christ in South Africa. Many of the outstanding workers in the different churches and missions, both ministers and laymen who have been used mightily by God, received their inspiration and spiritual equipment in these gatherings. One of the outstanding features of these Keswicks was the number who entered into a very definite experience of the fullness or baptism of the Holy Spirit, and reached a place of real victory and power over sin. Andrew insisted that the speakers be very clear-cut in their teaching and was careful to invite only those who fully concurred with the Convention position.

Because travel remained difficult and time-consuming, by popular demand arrangements were made for the holding of similar conferences in more than a half dozen other South African towns. Andrew always tried to work in harmony with the ministers of the various churches in any region. Not all accepted his spiritual teaching platform, but their relationships together were open and brotherly. One of the most argumentative and perhaps least sympathetic of the local ministers in a certain place, voiced himself: "Well, I do not accept Mr. Murray's teaching. But one is left in no doubt as to *what* he teaches; it is clear as daylight!"

One of Andrew's Keswick messages on the subject of the filling of the Holy Spirit is typical, revealing his clarity and boldness of teaching. His main points were:

"I *must* be filled. It is absolutely *necessary*.

"I *may* be filled. God has made it blessedly *possible*.

"I *would* be filled. It is eminently *desirable*.

"I *will* be filled. It is so blessedly *certain*."

Andrew's message was always simple: Come to Jesus; abide in Him; work through Him. Repeatedly he emphasized the little central word "in." "The two parts of the promise 'Abide *in* me and I *in* you' find their union in that significant little word. There is no more profound word in all of Scripture," he declared.

In the last years of his life Andrew became quite deaf, but remarkably he continued to be chairman of the Keswick Convention. He kept in touch with the proceedings by asking someone to give him running notes of the addresses.

The most active evangelistic outreach years of Andrew's ministry were from 1879 to 1891. Seven evangelistic campaigns were held in all parts of South Africa with Andrew as speaker. His congregation acknowledged his special gift and calling for evangelism and gladly granted him leave of absence for these revivals.

To find out how he could conduct such extensive campaigns (without any of the modern equipment, easy transportation, or sophisticated staff which our age considers essential), let us ask Andrew:

"How do you get ready for such meetings when you are invited to a certain church?"

"I instruct the minister of the congregation how best to kindle large expectations of what God is going to do in their midst. It is important that the audience be spiritually ripe to receive God's truth. I want him to urge believers to pray continuously and in faith not only for a general blessing, but for individuals whom God has laid on their hearts — family members, friends. At the same time, I enlist the prayer of other congregations in churches at large to bear up each evangelistic service in their intercession, so that it might please God to grant a rich harvest of souls."

"Does someone else take care of all your travel arrangements, so that you may devote yourself fully to the ministry?"

"No, I usually attend to the details of travel myself, both the stages of my itinerary and all the meeting schedules."

"Does everyone welcome such meetings?"

"Ah, no. There are prejudices to be removed, difficulties to be smoothed away, ignorance to be dispelled, and coldness and diffidence to be overcome."

"What particular objections might a minister have regarding a revival?"

"Some are not against special services as such, but they fear the 'after-meetings.' We are a very formal and ordered people in the Dutch Church. But I have learned from my friend D. L. Moody that these are absolutely essential to conserve the spiritual results and to strengthen the new babes. I tell them that it would be like breaking off the point of the arrow to stop short of that kind of follow-up."

In spite of superficial differences, his fellow ministers, in almost every case, were happy to welcome him and gave him cooperation; the audiences, too, were most receptive. To prepare for his meetings, Andrew usually sent ahead parcels of his latest books, usually twenty at a time, to serve as preparatory messages.

Random comments from letters by Andrew about a series of his meetings serve to provide us with a little flavor of his activities:

"I arrived after a rattling drive of twenty hours. . . ; the spiritual shaking here has been very real, but at first we felt like we were speaking against a dead wall. We are expecting large blessings. . . . Our services here are over, resulting in deep feeling among many, and open confession among some. We praise God . . . . I had hard work here, doing most of the talking, but the spiritual change here has so set me up that I hardly feel tired. God gives strength . . . . I feel one needs time to get more of God into one's life and work. Lord, teach us . . . . Such roads, truly like the Transvaal! This morning on awakening, for the first time I felt tired, but it is all right now . . . . Services began this afternoon in pouring rain. I am humbly asking the Father to command it to cease. . . . I have begun on the way to write a Dutch book on Hebrews, which I look to God to bless very much . . . . Testimonies here are in abundance and very clear, of blessings received by people who had long feared the Lord but had not known what salvation by faith was. And some twenty confessions of conversion . . . . Had some clear cases of entrance into light and joy, and in the next service a number of people came forward again. A young girls' prayer meeting has started, also a boys' .... Much proof of God's blessing on the services and so many testimonies to the effect: 'I thought I must be, or get, or do something. And now I see it was all wrong; I now trust the living Jesus.' The joy is great in many hearts. I meet a lot of people who are the fruit of former special services. . . . So the Lord proves the work is not in vain. To His name be the praise!"

As Andrew received warm hospitality wherever he went as an evangelist, he likewise extended a generous welcome to other evangelists who visited South Africa. Only a few might be mentioned: John R. Mott, F. B. Meyer, Spencer Walton, John McNeill, Mark Guy Pearse, Gipsy Smith, and Donald Fraser.

Dr. F. B. Meyer wrote of the courtesies shown him in South Africa which he recognized would not have been accorded him if Andrew had not come to welcome him upon arrival and to attend his meetings even when he was in his eighties. "It was of untold help that my earliest meetings should receive the endorsement and blessing of the recognized father and leader of the Dutch Church."

In spite of his advanced years, Andrew was always open to new means of sharing God's Word with the people. His interest was awakened upon hearing about "One-day Conferences" (two or three sessions in a particular church, but lasting a single day). This appealed to the limited strength of Andrew and he wrote a leaflet promoting the scheme, which was taken up by many churches. Subjects were suggested which would be of spiritual benefit to the congregation and which would enable the minister to know the needs and attitudes of his people better. When Andrew participated in them, though he was frail and thin, it was reported that he seemed, each time he ministered, to overcome his weakness and amazed all with his fire and energy.

In 1904 Andrew founded the Prayer Union, which was open to Christians who had pledged themselves to devote at least a quarter of an hour daily to praying for others and also for the furtherance of the Kingdom of Christ throughout the world. When Andrew died, the Union was called "The Andrew Murray Prayer Union" to serve as a lasting memorial to his influence as a man of prayer and his sincere pleas regarding the role and the power of prayer in the council of God. In later years this Union incorporated the Revival Union and the Abundant Life Movement.

In his closing years Andrew was described as "of medium height with spare frame, thin gray beard, hair that hung in great locks about his neck, and deep, mystic, hazel eyes." Until that accident in Natal which permanently injured his spine, his bearing was upright, his step rapid, and his frame so wiry that it could endure the greatest strain which circumstances or hard work could impose. That injury changed his figure into one which was stooped and had an almost deformed appearance. He eventually had to sit on a high stool while preaching, though this did not in the least affect his sincerity and passionate delivery.

Andrew's voice, even in old age, was full and resonant, and there was something peculiarly sincere and engaging in the heartiness of his greeting to all. He possessed an exceptionally keen memory, not merely for facts set down in books, but for matters which he had observed or which had been told him in years gone by. He was careful in attending to details, regular in hours of his daily schedule and in replying to correspondence, punctual in keeping appointments and settling accounts.

The ultra-sternness of the early days of his ministry had evolved into a gentle, open, loving quality that tempered all of his relations with people. He maintained a strong sense of humor, though he kept it under restraint because of his official public positions. It would break out at unexpected moments, however. Often it saved the day during tense times when he was moderator of the synod, to relieve and calm an excited assembly.

Andrew had a ready gift for having just the right illustration or anecdote at appropriate moments. As an example, after holding a series of gospel meetings at a village in the Free State, Andrew announced a "testimony meeting" before the country people would disperse to their farms again. To get the meeting started, he put to them the startling question, "What is the first sign of a man's having taken too much wine?" After a pause, he answered his own question: "Talkativeness!" "And now," he continued, "what should be the first sign of a man's having received a blessing from God at this conference? Why, talkativeness — not a convivial, but a spiritual talkativeness. For that is what the Apostle Paul says: 'Be not drunk with wine, but be filled with the Spirit, *speaking to one another. . . .*' "

During one of Andrew's evangelistic conferences in Natal, a certain speaker protested against the extravagant language of joy and praise and elation sed by some of the people who attended Holiness meetings.

Andrew replied tactfully, "Yes, some sincere and godly people, in the overflowing fullness of their experience of a new truth, may not always express themselves conservatively, or perhaps in the accustomed manner. But we must not reject the experience because of the expressions which may accompany it. That reminds me of the old days when we used to travel by ox-wagon. At the end of the day's journey, the first thing to be done was to light the fire, boil the water, and put in the meat. While we watched the cooking process, we saw the scum rise to the surface. Of course we skimmed it off and threw it away, but we did not throw away the meat!"

Naturally there were some who criticized Andrew's messages, but he always took care not to defend himself. Sometimes, of course, there were false reports that others wished to correct on his behalf out of their love and loyalty. On one such occasion, a close friend resented very strongly some damaging criticisms that were spoken concerning a published address of Andrew's. On his own, the friend prepared a vindication which he read to Andrew and asked his advice about publishing it.

"Do you think this reply will convince our critic?" Andrew asked.

"No, I don't suppose it will."

"Then what will be the use of publishing it? It will only lead to further controversy, from which nothing will be gained." The matter was dropped and left to the Lord.

His versatile interests were seen in the widely varied

aspects of life on which he touched. Total abstinence and church unification, faith healing and the Afrikaaner interests, may to the average man appear to be matters so remotely removed that only a miracle could join them. To Andrew it was nothing out of the ordinary to move from one to the other with the greatest of ease.

Andrew had no problem with integrating spiritual life and matters of the real world about him. They were all one to him. A certain Christian gentleman approached Andrew to discuss a business problem with him, but hesitated to do so because Andrew had, just a few minutes before, finished delivering a most spiritual address to a congregation. Andrew was so keenly attentive to the business immediately that the man was quite amazed.

"How can you manage, sir," he asked, "to turn with such ease from spiritual exhortation to practical business detail?"

"Why," said Andrew, "surely *this* is the Master's business as well as the other."

25

The Family Touch

The most familiar title for our subject was "Andrew Murray of Wellington." Andrew spent forty-six years of his ministry in this city as home base, living in two different homes: in the parsonage near the church for twenty-one years, until he passed it over to his associate pastor in 1892, and then in his personally built residence "Clairvaux," on a portion of ground belonging to the Training Institute. The latter was surrounded by buildings of the Institute at rather close quarters, but since it was on a little ridge the view of valley, gardens, vineyards, waving cornfields and Dutch homesteads — all fading away to the distant, lofty Drakenstein Mountains — justified its location.

It was on the broad stone veranda on the sunny north of the house that Andrew wrote his books, received his visitors, and transacted business when the weather was favorable. He never wearied of the quiet pastoral scene, remote from the dusty highways of life and the throb of the restless world.

All his life he had appreciated beauty, delighting in the sights and smells of gardens, particularly roses, which held for him memories of the gardening by Emma and himself no matter where they were in the pastorate. Purple lilacs reminded him of Scotland and his boyhood. When a vase full of violets was put upon his study table he would frequently lift it and draw a long whiff with evident enjoyment. The changing colors of nature caused him always to exclaim of the lavish goodness of God in making so much beauty for His creatures to enjoy.

Emma has been met throughout this story and described as a true life-partner — an affectionate, understanding wife, a faithful mother, one who was in closest sympathy with Andrew's work, who with joy and enthusiasm shared his congregational labors.

For about fifty years of his life one or more young people, chiefly boys, lived in the Murray parsonage, "adopted" unofficially as part of their family, being educated in the hope of supplying the need for Christian workers. It was wonderful to see how Emma opened her heart to these children. In her letters to her family one can hardly distinguish between her interest in the formation of the character of her own children and those living in their household.

Although their own family was so large that it might have fully occupied her, being a woman of culture and learning herself, she was involved in many of the educational and training ventures which were established through the years. In the early days at Bloemfontein she shouldered the care of the students at Grey College in connection with Andrew's rectorship. During the revival of 1860 she started a ladies' prayer meeting at Worcester, which continued as a spiritual force through many years. At Worcester and Cape Town she pioneered in enlisting children for work-circles for the missionary cause, and worked untiringly in the Sunday Schools. As her children grew up and she became more free, she was able to do even more.

Emma was intensely interested in the ministry with the Huguenot Seminary, the Missionary Training Institute, and Friedenheim, a successful training school for women workers. She helped to start a very successful industrial school for poor white girls; she was president from the beginning of the Women's Missionary Union, whose marvelous growth and wide influence were due largely to her unceasing labors and wise counsel.

Emma's disposition was such that a young seminarian who lived in their home for an extended period complimented her by saying, "She was such a gracious, wifely, motherly person that *not* to be in harmony with her would be self-condemnation."

As Andrew and Emma advanced in years they also grew wiser, but in many ways they kept an almost youthful enthusiasm for new ideas and interests wider than those of their immediate surroundings. Emma's belief in her husband was always expressed. Andrew could count on his wife's alert, intelligent response to any of his new schemes and on her help and energy in carrying them out. Many felt that without Emma to spur him on, it is doubtful that Andrew could have produced the enormous output of religious writing which he did in his busiest years.

When the Murrays moved to Wellington, they had nine children. The two youngest died the following year, but in 1873 another son, the last of the family, was born. Most of the child training fell to Emma, since Andrew was away on evangelistic missions so much of the time. She did an exemplary job, and drew to herself the lasting love and appreciation of her children.

Eight children lived to maturity — four sons and four daughters. Their eldest son, Howson Rutherfoord, was the first of these to die, at the young age of twenty-three. Not being a strong lad, he had been unable to continue studies, so entered business with his uncle in Cape Town, where he died unexpectedly while his parents were absent on ministry in the Transvaal.

Their eldest daughter, Emmie, joined the Salvation Army, reaching the rank of staff-captain, and served until she resigned to become director of a Christian institution for the rescue of young girls and unfortunate women. Mary, the second daughter, became a missionary among African tribes. The third daughter, Catherine Margaret (Kitty), pursued an educational career and occupied important positions in schools, first as principal of the branch Huguenot Seminary at Bethlehem and later at Graaff-Reinet. The youngest daughter, Annie, was Andrew's faithful and zealous private secretary and traveling companion for his last twenty years.

John and Charles also became missionaries among the tribes, Charles later taking a pastorate after his wife died in the malarial climate of Nyasaland. In his later years, he again became a missionary at Mochudi. The second eldest son, Andrew Haldane, was a most gifted and intellectual lad, having studied at Cambridge and returned to the Cape to pass his examination for the degree of M.A. He became a most diligent director of schools until he changed his occupation to engage in farming in Graaff-Reinet. A highly respected member of the community, he became a representative in the

House of Assembly. When World War I broke out, he volunteered as a private for the East African campaign, rose to be lieutenant, but then was killed in action in 1916 at the age of fifty in an attempt to save the life of a wounded fellow-countryman. He left behind a wife and three children.

Through Andrew's initiative, it became a habit among the different family members to intercede for each other every Sunday evening, and sing the hymn that was associated with the elder Murray's departure from Scotland: "O God of Bethel, by whose hand Thy people still are fed." Family reunions of the many scattered Murray clans in South Africa were held a number of times.

In 1906 one reunion was recorded at which there were sixty-eight descendants present. Andrew himself was there and refreshed the memories of the younger generation about the pioneer days of his father. "Our father came to this country a solitary man and God has made of him a great host."

A significant cause to praise God was brought forth, "that of all of Papa Murray's grandchildren, there was *not one* of whom we had cause to be ashamed." Special prayer was made for the fourth generation, that they, too, might choose the God of their fathers as their God. "You will not play football less successfully for choosing to serve God," they were reminded.

A nephew, Andrew Charles Murray, cautioned the group that privileges bring obligations. "We are very highly privileged in being heirs to the prayers of our parents, grandparents and great-grandparents, but we should in turn pray for *our* children. They may change their names by marriage or go to the ends of the earth, but they cannot escape the mark placed upon them, for in their veins flows the blood of generations of praying ancestors."

The latest reunion, to the writer's knowledge, was held on August 25, 1950 when eighty-six mainly direct descendants met in Andrew Murray Hall in Stellenbosch. Among them were a number of octogenarians who remembered "the early days." On that occasion many of the third, fourth, and fifth generation met one another, some for the first time. A moving account of this gathering ended with the report that they were all led in a simple prayer of rededication, in the hope that they, too, might do their utmost to follow in the footsteps of their forefathers, to bring glory to the Kingdom of God and honor to His name.

Many men have one face toward the outside world and another toward their family and home. They can be merry and agreeable enough with strangers, but at home it is a different matter. One of the young men who was studying for the ministry stayed with the Murrays for an extended time and observed the following about Andrew:

"He was a very highly strung man. His preaching was so enthusiastic; his gesticulation so unrestrained that he was wearing himself out and the doctor ordered him to sit while preaching. . . . Such an output of nervous energy might well mean some reaction at home, some irritation with his wife, some unevenness toward his children, some caprice with the stranger within his gates. *But now!* I never knew him thrown off his balance . . . . He was solid gold throughout."

One of his biographers, W. M. Douglas, said he wrote as one who "had ample opportunity to judge" Andrew's temperament because he worked in a mission organization with him, was both his guest and host, a fellow traveler to conventions, and was with him in committee meetings and under trying circumstances. He bore tribute that —"I have never seen the slightest impatience, irritability or anger in him. To me he has seemed the loveliest and humblest of men, the embodiment of holiness as well as its exponent. I admired his consistency and exalted spirituality. My ministry was transformed largely by his books thirty-five years ago in England."

Andrew practiced what he preached, particularly regarding prayer. A friend recalled what a perfectly natural way he brought everything to the Lord in prayer. One day there had been an argument with another man who was helping with special evangelistic services. The man was rather bent on having his own way in a matter, and it was being discussed at dinner ... All at once Andrew said, "Let us ask God!" and all knelt immediately at the table while he prayed. Apparently the man felt rather ashamed of himself, and when everyone arose, he did not pursue the argument. Andrew had a wonderful tenderness and skill in dealing wisely even with overbearing people.

Andrew's daughter Emmie recollected that in the earlier days of her father's ministry, although he romped happily with them at play, yet the children feared him also because he was so stern. But after his time of enforced silence due to his throat problem, his relationship with everyone seemed to change remarkably, almost to reflect a different personality.

"At that time God came so near to Father and he saw more clearly the meaning of a life of full surrender and simple faith. Then he began to show in all relationships that constant tenderness, unruffled lovingkindness, and unselfish thought for others which increasingly characterized his life thereafter. At the same time, Father lost nothing of his strength or determination."

Three grandsons, the sons of his son John, spent ten years of their lives at "Clairvaux" for their education. Andrew's family never regarded him as a plaster saint upon a pedestal, but a very warm and understanding individual, totally approachable, whom they dearly loved and from whom they could learn much about nearly everything. Andrew's grandchildren and the children of nephews and nieces always had a welcome at the home of Grandpa, or "Oupa" as they addressed him in Dutch. He would spend much time chatting with them on their level, holding the young ones on his lap, reading to them, and letting them romp with his stout ebony walking stick for a hobby horse.

Andrew walked with God, but he also walked joyfully among his family and his fellow men.

26

Not Sunset But Promotion

A friend recollected that Andrew's power for work was something unusual, even with advancing age and intensive travel. One day after a prolonged trip together, Emma said to him, "I think we ought to go home now; we are getting old."

He replied, "Speak for yourself only, Mother. I don't want to die yet; there is still too much to be done."

At a certain public meeting where people were present who did not ordinarily go to religious meetings, a lady who did not know Andrew saw him ascend the pulpit steps, frail and gray and stooped.

"Who is that old man?" she asked. "What a shame to make him go up those steps to preach!"

A friend of Andrew's sitting next to her thought to himself, My dear lady, do you have a surprise coming tonight!

As Andrew got up to speak he seemed to grow tall and majestic, and he spoke loudly and forcefully on behalf of a new mission work opening up in the Sudan. "Forward!" was his cry. So surprised was the lady that her pity gave way to reverence.

245

"What a voice for such a body!" she exclaimed. Clear as a bell, with irresistible power and command, Andrew proclaimed God's words in tones which knew no hesitation or defeat.

People in Europe and America were as impressed by Andrew's quiet humility and manner, as he met and conversed with them, as they were enthralled by his impassioned utterances. He did have severe critics, but even they admired his Christlike bearing as he heard and replied to their objections. It was written of him: "As the tree that bears the most fruit bends lowest and almost breaks under its own weight, so the holier he grew in advancing years and the more famous he became, the humbler he appeared and the more his very face shone with the glory within."

Another student who lived with the Murrays commented, "There was no mid-autumn spoiling of the crop; but the whole matured harvest was fully gathered in without shortcoming and without loss — and what a harvest!"

"I saw him five months before his death, and his venerable face shone like Alpine mountains with the glow of the setting sun, so radiant, so benignant with the purity within," wrote a friend.

On his last birthday he was asked whether he felt any disappointment that God allowed his lameness and deafness to keep him from a more active life.

"It is a kindly dispensation of my Father's providence," he replied contentedly. "God has shut me out from the life of ceaseless activity which I led in former years, and shut me in to greater quiet in which I can give more time to meditation and prayer. In the solitude and silence the Lord speaks precious messages to me which I try to pass on to others through my writing."

His exhortation to others on his last birthday was, "Children of God, let your Father lead you. Think not of what you can do, but of what God can do in you and through you."

"What are you doing sitting so quietly in the sun, Father?" his daughter once inquired.

"I am asking God to show me the need of the Church and to give me a message to meet the need. Children, remember to bask in the love of God as we bask in the sunshine of a winter's day."

There was no generation gap between Andrew and the youth, even in his final years. All the societies that worked among the young had a special place in his heart and he gave them his full support. He prayed and yearned to lead young people to a full surrender of their lives and their powers to the Lord Jesus Christ. The Christian Endeavor movement was one of his keenest interests. He became and remained president of the society in Wellington for the remainder of his life. Both English and Dutch branches were established in South Africa. It was to this organization that Andrew dedicated his book *The Mystery of the True Vine.*

The Students' Christian Association was another of Andrew's concerns. This group united with two others and formed the nucleus of the Volunteer Movement for those who felt the call of the Lord to missionary work. His joy was great when his youngest son and two nephews joined this group and went to Nyasaland.

Andrew so loved the young people that he always welcomed them in for a quiet talk, with life-changing influences upon them. One of the younger members of his family remarked about the aged Andrew, "Uncle Andrew never grows old." He was the embodiment of the description of the Psalmist, "He will still yield fruit in old age and shall be full of sap and very green" (Ps. 92:14, ERV).

In Andrew's eightieth year, as a result of the establishment of the Laymen's Missionary Union, a missionary crusade was inaugurated with the weight of the responsibility and work falling upon him. He traveled far and wide through the country giving rousing addresses on behalf of missions. People often wondered how he, such an old man, could stand it. One of his daughters warned, "Father, you will die in the train on your strenuous travels!"

"No, my child," he answered, "I shall not. I shall die in my bed." And this proved to be true.

The last few years before his death he took a long tour of up to five weeks once a year, and shorter journeys between, giving many addresses along the way to churches, conventions, mission groups, ministers' meetings, and congresses. At one point his daughter records that he preached twenty-eight times in twelve days, and it was *preaching!* Afterward, from a full heart he would pour out praise and thanksgiving for traveling mercies, and intercessions on behalf of the work and for the friends whom he had met on the tours. One of his ministerial brethren remarked, "He never repeats himself." One secret of his power was that every message was newly received for the occasion; he did not offer stale bread to hungry souls.

At home between tours he did not collapse or let down but was just as energetic as when with the public. He usually dictated letters and books both in the morning and afternoon, but was always ready to meet any friends who came to see him, not considering them interruptions. He would always have prayer with them, on the broad veranda in front of his study which was his favorite place to sit and pray and meditate when not writing.

World War I caused Andrew much sorrow, both for the turmoil of the nations and for his loved ones who were involved. He was interested in the war news day by day and took many illustrations from it for his messages. He was excited to learn about the development of new technologies like submarines and machine guns and "fights in air ships."

Commenting on his manner during old age, a member of his family wrote, "Father speaks very quietly now, with very little exertion, but with great spiritual power. His seems like a voice on the verge of eternity, of one just ready to go on living while God wills. He is glad to live to deliver God's messages, but he talks little, and conserves all his strength for work. Yet he has never been more bright and joyous in his whole life, so restful and peaceful. The world and all its interests seem in abeyance, and God's Kingdom and its concerns absorb his thoughts and heart. He has never lost touch with the life that is around him."

Andrew had been suffering from hardening of the arteries for some years, and late in 1916 he suffered an attack of influenza which left him very weak. One of his biographers describes it as "God gently taking down the pins of the earthly tabernacle." It was during his slow recovery that the news came of the death of his eldest son in action on the battlefield. For some weeks the news was kept from him because of his weakness, but when he was informed, he bore his deep sorrow with Christian courage.

During his recovery he loved to sit on the veranda of his shore cottage at Kalk Bay and look out over the sea.

"Just look at the sea — what beautiful waves! How full the sea appears to be today, just like the love of God, so boundless, so vast, so free, so full. Can we look upon this beautiful ocean and doubt the love of God? Does not each wave seem to say to us, 'Have faith in God, He is so wonderful, so mighty; He is the Almighty.'

"Annie — where is Annie? I want to write so that all may know about this wonderful mighty God, so loving, so tender, so unutterably worthy to be trusted and believed in by perishing mortals who are so unable to grasp His greatness and majesty and might."

During the nights when he could not sleep he poured out his heart in prayer for ministers, for God's people, and for his country. "Pray, pray, pray for the nation that it might be a righteous nation," he would often plead.

His mind was always on the next book he wanted to write. When a friend wrote about his little child dying, the word "promotion" was used. Andrew's fertile mind was sparked: "That word 'promotion' has given me a thought for a new book. Promotion is the *favor of God*. So I will write very simply how we may obtain it, so that the most ignorant can understand it. First I will write about the favor of our great God; second, that we obtain it only through Christ; and lastly, that it is applied by the Holy Spirit."

As the aged Apostle John in his writings, so Andrew's thoughts centered on the *love of God* as he prepared to embark on the next step of his eternal life. Just before his death he said, "The great and wonderful God wants to live out His life in us. He can do so only as we *dwell in love.* We can dwell in love only as Christ lives out His life in us, when we are fully yielded to Him. Let us then surrender ourselves to Him that more of God's great and wonderful life may be lived in us."

On the last evening of his life, preparing for bed, he said, "We have such a great and glorious God that we ought to be always rejoicing in Him." Then he prayed, "Oh! ever-blessed and glorious God, satisfy us with Thy mercy that we may rejoice and be glad in Thee all our days. Satisfy me that I may rejoice and be glad *always* in Thee." He literally died in communication with his Heavenly Father.

The final sentences of his life were to his daughter. "Have faith in God, my child. Do not doubt Him," and "God is worthy of trust." On the eighteenth of January, 1917, at the age of eighty-eight, Andrew Murray peacefully met his beloved Lord face to face.

The day of his funeral, shops and places of business were closed and all Wellington assembled in the great church to testify of their love and respect for the man of God who was known in so many of the churches of Christendom. His burial was in the churchyard near the Dutch Reformed Church, the grave being immediately to the right of the main entrance. Telegrams poured in from the highest officials of the land and from abroad.

There were countless tributes to Andrew but only a few sentences will be selected to sum up his life: "Andrew Murray never sought fame. Apparently he was a man without ambition — except the ambition so characteristic of St. Paul, 'to preach the gospel' and 'to be well-pleasing to God.' In the days of his prime, his appeals stirred thousands, for his influence in the pulpit was magnetic. His tremendous earnestness swayed men's minds as the wind sways the cornfield.... He was essentially a man of prayer, and at the same time, a man of affairs. The eternal world was to him an intense reality, not a matter of speculation: things spiritual, in his case, dominated the temporal. Prayer, to Andrew Murray, meant unbroken communion with the Unseen and intercession for others, fellowship in feeling and suffering with the Church of God in all portions of the globe. . . . Every new book he wrote was welcomed because it was fresh and stimulating. . . . Life for him meant simply that all activity was to be permeated and purified by the sense of the Eternal presence.... He was always pressing on — another mission given by God to perform, a message still to proclaim, a book or two still to be written. Some years ago a friend approached him with the request, 'Will you not give us some of your reminiscences?' The answer was characteristic: 'I have far better things to do than to talk and write about myself.' A mystic, a prophet, and a humble-minded follower of the Master, his has been a full life. . . ."

Because the passion of Andrew's life had been to share with others through his writings that which he had found to be most precious, people throughout the world have received fullness in Christ. Andrew Murray left a rich spiritual legacy of which we are joyful heirs!

APPENDIX

The major books of Andrew Murray which are currently in print in English are listed in alphabetical order by title. Synopses and notes on the background of their writing are included where possible. Cross references are provided to chapters in this book which give additional information.

Murray did not write all of his books from start to finish as intended books; some were reprints of articles that appeared in the official magazine of the Dutch Reformed Church of South Africa — first known as *De Gereformeerde Kerkbode* (1849 to 1879), then called *De Christen* (1879 to 1883), and later named *De Kerkbode* (1884 to 1933); others were compilations, by Murray or others, of his messages on certain themes.

Chapter 23 of this volume is a full discussion of Andrew Murray's creativeness, writing habits, techniques, and the effect of his publications on the Christian world of his day. In various other chapters, reference is made to events in his writing career.

Murray's most fruitful year of writing was 1895, when no fewer than sixteen of his publications appeared. Though seven were only short addresses of fewer than ten pages each, nine were substantial books averaging 135 pages. He was fond of the format of thirty-one or fifty-two chapters which could be read daily for a month or weekly for a year. In the last five years of his life he was particularly inclined to a "pocket" series, of which twelve booklets were published.

Abide in Christ

Written in 1864, this was one of Murray's earliest works. Subtitled "Thoughts on the Blessed Life of Fellowship with the Son of God," it was written in the old Dutch parsonage at Worcester as a manual to guide the many converts from the great revival of 1860. Within four years, more than 40,000 copies were sold. Eighteen years later Murray issued it as the first of his English books. The teachings were designed to prevent the all-too-frequent falling short of the glorious life of full salvation after the new birth. The format is daily meditations for one month on the depths of what Jesus meant in John 15:4 concerning abiding, and the emphasis is that it is most certainly within the reach of every new believer. (See also Chapters 10, 11, 17, and 19 of this book for background.)

* * * * *

Absolute Surrender

Published originally in 1895, these nine chapters are an exposition of what the author believed was the one great need of the Church and each believer. He summarizes: "Your God in Heaven answers the prayers which you have offered for blessing on yourselves and for blessing on those around you by this one demand: Are you willing to surrender yourself absolutely into His hands?" (See also Chapters 10 and 11 of this book for background.)

Aids to Devotion

First published in 1909, subtitled "Thoughts on the Holy Spirit in the Epistle to the Ephesians," this was originally a series of articles under that title written as helps for the quiet hour and printed in the *Lovedale Christian Express*. The purpose is that the believer might "realize what the standard of the true Christian life is as it is set before us in Ephesians, and what absolute, divine assurance it gives us that God is able and willing to make all that it contains true in our experience."

* * * * *

Be Perfect

Published originally in 1893, it was begun at the Murrays' favorite vacation spot at Kalk Bay, on the last day of their annual vacation one year. Everyone was involved with last minute preparations for departure, and there was Andrew, oblivious to all the confusion, sitting contentedly at a window overlooking the sea, quietly thrilled with a fresh message from the Lord and a commission to deliver it in print. In thirty-one chapters the author traces the term "perfect" through the Scriptures, seeking to understand the correct meaning from the context. He concludes that there is a perfection of which Scripture speaks which is possible and attainable, in fact, is a command to be obeyed with our whole heart. It is obtained only by yielding oneself to the leading of the Holy Spirit so that God may accomplish that perfection in us.

The Blood of the Cross

This book contains the last ten discourses of Murray on this subject, the first fifteen of which are published in the book *The Power of the Blood of Jesus*. This subject first gripped his attention on a trip to Europe, and on his return to South Africa in 1883 he gave messages on The Blood during Passion Week to his congregation at Wellington. This is a brilliantly researched, spiritually moving study of the power of the blood of Christ, the deepest mystery of redemption. The author asserts that there can be no freedom of approach to God, nor fellowship with Him, apart from the truly vital and powerful experience of the efficacy of the blood of Christ, and skillfully leads the reader to a full awareness of what that blood actually signifies.

* * * * *

Confession and Forgiveness

Originally published in 1895 under the title *Have Mercy Upon Me*, this book examines Psalm 51 phrase by phrase, revealing the classically simple message of God's forgiveness.

* * * * *

Daily Thoughts on Holiness from Andrew Murray

A recently edited (1977) compilation of devotional readings for every day of the year (actually dated). The excerpts are taken from twelve of Murray's best known books and each reading is annotated with the source and page number.

Day by Day with Andrew Murray

Originally published in 1899 as *The Andrew Murray Year Book*, it contains paragraph-length extracts from twenty-six of his works, one for each day of the year. The theme which M. J. Shepperson, the compiler, selected to tie these thoughts together is "that our Lord Jesus is willing to be far more to us than we know. All that we have enjoyed of Him is only a beginning."

* * * * *

Divine Healing

First published in English in 1900, each of the thirty-one chapters are based on a scripture related to healing. (Refer to Chapters 17 and 18 of this book for the background events of Murray's life related to this subject.) Murray regarded this book as the testimony to his faith in divine healing. "I can no longer keep silence," he wrote, "that this truth is in perfect accord with Holy Scripture and essential for every one who would see the Lord manifest His power and His glory in the midst of His children."

* * * * *

Freedom From a Self-Centered Life

Subtitled "Dying to Self," first published in 1898, these are selections from the writings of William Law, edited by Murray. In form it consists of four dialogues between various individuals, interspersed with Murray's illuminating comments. The chief thought is how to live in Christ above the average state of failure in which most believers are found, which has its roots in the self-life. (See Chapter 23 for an evaluation of Law's theology; also see the Introduction of *Wholly for God*.)

* * * * *

The Full Blessing of Pentecost

Subtitled "The One Thing Needful," it was first published in 1907. The purpose of the author was to urge believers to lay aside everything to obtain this experience of power. This book expresses intense fervor of writing surpassing any of his other works. The simple but most serious message is that "men ought everywhere to seek with one accord and with their whole heart to be filled with the Spirit of God." Murray sought to emphasize that the filling with the Holy Spirit is for every believer to live in entirely and unceasingly; without it neither a Christian nor a church can ever live or work as God desires; so few have it or even seek it; God is waiting to bestow it; our self-life and the world hinder it; we obtain it by yielding all of ourselves for this pearl of great price. Relating it to missions, Murray writes with all the fiery energy of his lifelong conviction, "To know what Pentecost means, to have its faith and its spirit, is the only power to evangelize the world in this generation. The pentecostal commission can only be carried out by a pentecostal church in pentecostal power!" (See also Chapters 19 and 21 for background.)

Helps to Intercession

Published originally in 1898 in London under the title *Pray Without Ceasing,* these thirty-one short meditations on scriptures relating to aspects of prayer aid the reader to pinpoint his own special petitions. The format for each day's reading is divided into two parts, "What to Pray" and "How to Pray," with space for personal prayer requests and notes.

* * * * *

The Holiest of All

This is a devotional exposition of Hebrews in 130 chapters, originally published in 1894. Topics cover: the Presence of God; the Sphere of Christ's Ministry; Heaven and Our Life and Service on Earth. The author's purpose was to show "how the Holy Spirit reveals the way into the Holiest as opened by the blood of Christ and invites us by faith in Christ to have our life there. It is as we yield our hearts to the leading of the Spirit to know Christ and look at Him, and believe in what is revealed, that the Spirit can take possession of us."

* * * * *

Holy in Christ

Published originally in 1887, it is the result of careful theological study coupled with warm evangelistic fervor. Subtitled "Thoughts on the Calling of God's

Children to be Holy as He is Holy," the book comprises thirty-one readings for a month, exploring the possibility of the believer living the reality of a seemingly impossible command and expectation of his Lord. The author traces through the Scriptures what God meant to convey by the term "holy" and its centrality in Jesus. Murray has carefully explained for us "the conviction that *we must be holy*, the knowledge of *how we are to be holy*, the joy that *we may be holy*, the faith that *we can be holy*." (See Chapters 19 and 20 of this book for background.)

* * * * *

How to Raise Your Children for Christ

Published in 1886, this book was one of Murray's earlier works, first in Dutch and later in English under the title *What Manner of Child Shall This Be?* It is also known as *The Children for Christ*. Its fifty-two short chapters deal with almost every aspect of child-raising. At Bloemfontein, and later at Worcester, Murray began the custom of monthly baptismal services when he would preach directly to the parents on this subject. Concerning his philosophy of training children in the Christian faith, he wrote, ". . . Surely it is obtainable, that instead of parental piety being diluted in children — this is so often spoken of as what we must expect — each succeeding generation of a God-fearing family ought to rise higher and higher. . . . The faith and the simplicity required for training children would perhaps be better training for the ministry than much that we consider great." Besides dealing with the principles of training, Murray set forth examples from the Old and New Testaments concerning children: bringing them to the Lord and helping them grow in faith. (See Chapters 6, 7 and 23 of this book for background.)

* * * * *

Humility

Twelve messages published first in 1895, directing attention to the humility that becomes us as those who have been created by God and which is indispensable for the fullness of the Christian life. "Pride must die in you, or nothing of Heaven can live in you. Look not at pride only as an unbecoming attitude, nor at humility only as a decent virtue: for the one is death, and the other is life; the one is all Hell, the other is all Heaven . . . . It is only in the possession of God that I lose myself." (See Chapter 10 of this book for background.)

* * * * *

The Inner Chamber and the Inner Life

Published originally in 1905, this book emphasizes the daily need of retirement and quiet for secret intercourse with God. The neglect of this holy habit is the "root disease" from which thousands of believers are suffering, which explains the feebleness of their Christian life. Most of the chapters were first published in *The South African Pioneer.* Among the topics considered are: The true spirit of prayer; the devotional reading of God's Word; the fellowship with God for which these are meant and by which alone they bring a blessing; the spiritual life which they are meant to strengthen and fit for daily duty in intercourse with the world; the service for the Kingdom of God in soul-winning and intercession. All of these truths, Murray claims, have their share in making our devotions a source of joy and strength.

* * * * *

Jesus Christ: Prophet/Priest

Four addresses delivered by Murray at the Mildmay Conference at Barnet, near London, in 1895. Topics cover: Our Prophet, The Completion of the Priesthood, Our Way into the Holiest, and The Food of the Soul.

* * * * *

The Key to the Missionary Problem

(See Chapter 22 of this book for a complete background of its writing and its effect upon Christians of his day.)

* * * * *

Let Us Draw Nigh

Published originally in 1894, these meditations on Hebrews 10:19-25 are twelve chapters from the larger book *The Holiest of All*, which is a comprehensive devotional exposition of the whole book of Hebrews.

"This selected passage constitutes the very core of the Epistle, a summary of what had been taught in its first or doctrinal part, and indicates the chief thoughts which are to be enforced in the second half . . . , the theme being, 'Let us draw nigh.' The state of those to whom Hebrews was written was just what we find in the churches of our day: a lack of steadfastness, of growth, and of power which arises from our not knowing Jesus aright . . . ."

* * * * *

Like Christ

This is a companion volume and sequel to *Abide in Christ*, issued in English in 1884. Two years later 19,000 copies had been sold. Thirty-one daily meditations for a month draw a portrait of Christ "to show how, in the reality of His human life, we have an exact pattern of what the Father wants us to be . . . . This is no mere ideal or human imitation, but *through the power of the Holy Spirit* is a most blessed reality." Murray urges us to "gaze and gaze again, worship and adore, and the more we see Him as He is, the more like Him we must become . . . by letting the heavenly likeness reflect itself and shine out in our life among our fellow-men. This is what we have been redeemed for, and let this be what we live for." (See also Chapter 17 of this book for background.)

The Lord's Table

Published originally in 1897, it was written as a help to the right observance of the Holy Communion. Murray recommended concerning its study: "Christians, give yourselves, give your Lord, time to transfer His heavenly thoughts to your inner, spiritual life; meditate on the portion for the day and appropriate it, not just read it." The format is in three parts: Meditations for each day of the week before the celebration; Ten meditations on the details of the Sacrament for the morning of that Lord's Day; Meditations for each day of the week after the Communion. (See also Chapter 13 of this book for background.)

* * * * *

The Master's Indwelling

Published originally in 1895, this book points out the difference between the life the average believer has been leading and the life that is abundantly available in the Spirit. It is designed to help the reader get out of the wilderness of defeat and into the Canaan of victory, with very practical instructions on how to make the change.

* * * * *

Money

First published in 1897 in London, this book gives Scriptural principles for stewardship of worldly possessions and counsel as to our attitude toward all things which are committed to us by God for His Kingdom.

* * * * *

The New Life

Published first in 1891, this book was written as Murray traveled between meetings. Its purpose was to provide a brief manual on basic Christianity for new Christians. In a format of fifty-two chapters for a whole year's meditations, the six leading thoughts of the new life are dealt with: the Word of God; the Son, the gift of the Father; sin; faith; the Holy Spirit; and the holy life. Each chapter is amply fortified with Scripture references which the new convert is urged to diligently look up. Questions and comments on the text are included, and a related prayer to guide the new believer is part of each meditation.

* * * * *

The Power of the Blood of Jesus

On Murray's voyage to Europe in 1882 he meditated much on the expression "There is power in the blood" and recalled the famous hymn in which the words are repeated over and over. The more he meditated, the more he inquired, in the spirit of prayer: What is this power and why has it this power? The following year, upon his return, he decided to give the answer to the question in a series of fifteen addresses delivered in his church during the season of preparation for Easter. Five more messages were subsequently added, and the whole was first published in a Christian magazine. Andrew maintained that the spiritual experimental power of the blood is absolutely necessary for the soul's conscious and joyous fellowship with God as well as for the attaining of holiness.

This book contains the first ten messages on the blood and the second ten are published in the book *The Blood of the Cross.*

* * * * *

POCKET COMPANION SERIES

Because of the titles, this is often popularly called the "Secret Series." It consists of twelve short booklets of thirty-one meditations each, on Murray's most prominent themes: They are, in order of writing:
The Secret of Intercession
The Secret of Adoration
The Secret of the Faith Life
The Secret of Inspiration
The Secret of the Abiding Presence
The Secret of United Prayer
The Secret of Fellowship
The Secret of the Cross
The Secret of Brotherly Love
The Secret of Power from on High
The Secret of Christ Our Life
The Secret of the Throne of Grace
(See Chapter 23 for background.)

The Power of the Spirit

These are selections from the writings of William Law, edited by Andrew Murray. First published in 1896, this book is addressed first of all to clergy and those in positions of Christian leadership, "that they do not miss that which is the most essential part of their message and work — the power of the Spirit of God in and through us." Murray indicates in his extensive preface the differences between his evangelical position and Law's tenets, so that the reader may have spiritual discernment and at the same time benefit deeply from the insights of the writer.

* * * * *

The Prayer Life

Early in 1912 a ministerial conference was called at Stellenbosch and attended by about .200 ministers, missionaries, and theological students. The purpose was to explore the reasons for the low state of spiritual life which marked the Church — universal and local. Those who participated searched their hearts in God's presence and He spoke to many of them, effecting confession, repentance, and restoration. Murray came out strongly with his conviction that one of the deepest roots of the weakness of the Church and its leadership was the sin of prayerlessness. His messages on that subject were first published in Dutch, later in English in this volume, so that its central thrust — that in spiritual work *everything depends on prayer* — could reach a larger audience through the printed page. (See Chapter 13 of this book for background.)

* * * * *

The School of Obedience

Published originally in 1898, this book of eight chapters is dedicated to all Christian students. Among the chief topics that Murray sought to emphasize are that God asks, requires and expects entire, day-by-day obedience of every believer; the enabling comes from the gift of His Son and the Holy Spirit; it is accomplished by absolute surrender to a life of abiding communion.

* * * * *

The Spirit of Christ

Published first in 1888, these thirty-one chapters for each day of the month comprise extensive studies from the Scriptures on major aspects of the Holy Spirit and His indwelling in the believer and the Church. There are seventeen detailed and enriching notes constituting the last quarter of the book; these deal in greater depth and doctrinal background with the topics considered in the major part of the text. (See also Chapters 10 and 19 of this book for background.)

The Spiritual Life

Murray did not write this book in the sense of deliberately setting out to produce a publication. He came to America in the summer of 1895 and was invited to speak in many illustrious pulpits. So many had already been helped through his previous writings that, when he gave a series of lectures to the students at the Moody Bible Institute in Chicago, it was urged that the stenographic reports of those messages be compiled into a book. This was done with Murray's permission and revision, and this book is the result.

* * * * *

The State of the Church

This book was written in 1911 when Murray was 83, in response to the Edinburgh World Missionary Conference. It was called "a book too faithful to be popular," and yet it became prominent because of its incisiveness in pointing out the lack of conversions, the striking decline of church membership, and the lack of spiritual vitality in the Church universal and local. Murray explained that he was not belittling the Church, but sounding the trumpet call to seven times more prayer that the Church might be healed of its chronic spiritual weakness. He powerfully reiterated that "the Church of today [his day and ours] as a whole is suffering from the lack of one thing only: the heavenly enduement of power which made the whole apostolic Church triumphant — the pentecostal Spirit." (See also Chapter 22 of this book for background.)

The True Vine
(sometimes titled *The Mystery of the True Vine*)

It was published originally in 1897 in a format of thirty-one meditations on John 15:1-16, "as a help to young Christians to take up that position in which the Christian life must be a success." From the vineyards that surrounded the Murray home at Wellington, and from studying the principal livelihood of the farmers in his parish, he received inspiration for this book, which, with additional thoughts, were later collected into a larger volume entitled *The Fruit of the Vine*. Murray also had an old vine stump which lay upon his study table during the summer of 1897. We can imagine him meditating on its rough, brown, shapelessness day after day as he prayed and prepared messages for his people. This book was dedicated to young people, and specifically to the members of the Society for Christian Endeavor throughout the world. (See also Chapters 13 and 26 for background.)

* * * * *

The Two Covenants

Published first in 1898 and subtitled "The Second Blessing," these eighteen meditations attempt to show "what exactly the blessings are that God has covenanted to bestow on us; what the Covenant assures us will be fulfilled; what the hold on God Himself is which it thus gives us; and what the conditions are for the full and continual experience of its blessings." Six discourses are appended, dealing with these topics: The Second Blessing; The Law Written in the Heart; George Muller and His Second Conversion; Canon Battersby; Nothing of Myself; and The Whole Heart.

* * * * *

Waiting on God

Mr. Murray prefaced the book in 1895 with the comments: "At all our conventions and assemblies too little time is given to waiting on God. Is He not willing to put things right in His own divine way? Has the life of God's people reached the utmost limit of what God is willing to do for them? Surely not. We want to wait on Him; to put away our experiences, however blessed they have been; our conceptions of truth, however sound and Scriptural; our plans, however needful and suitable they appear; and give God time and place to show us what *He* could do, what He *will* do. God has new developments and new resources. He can do new things, unheard-of things, hidden things. Let us enlarge our hearts and not limit Him . . . ." The book is arranged in thirty-one chapters for a month's readings. (See also Chapters 14 and 21 of this book for background.)

Wholly for God

These 110 separate short selections from the writings of William Law were edited by Murray in 1893. They span the entire spectrum of the spiritual life and its development. "I know of no writer who equals Law in the clearness and the force with which the claims of God on man are asserted. God is all; God must have all; God alone must work all: round these central truths all his teaching gathers." It was because the writings of Law in the early 1700's "were not at once easily apprehended," Murray explains, "that I have thought it to be of help to give such extracts from his books as would bring his more direct teachings on the spiritual life within the reach of all." But because some of Law's earlier works were controversial and theologically incomplete, it is essential for the reader to note carefully the author's twenty-two page Introduction for proper discernment and appreciation of Law's writings. (See also Chapter 23 of this book for background.)

* * * * *

With Christ in the School of Prayer
(sometimes titled *The School of Prayer*)

It was published first in 1885 and subtitled "Thoughts on Our Training for the Ministry of Intercession." When the Dutch original was published, a fellow minister wrote, "Oh, why didn't the author give us this book twenty-five years ago? It is a perfect treasury; and if Mr. Murray had published nothing else, our country would have owed him a great debt of gratitude." This book was the outgrowth of a ministerial conference at George on that subject. Afterward, Murray's meditations on prayer so engrossed him that he wrote this book piecemeal while traveling from town to town for special services. It includes an appendix chapter on George Muller's life and the secret of his power in prayer. Arranged in thirty-one chapters, the progressive teachings of Christ in regard to prayer are studied. Famed Dr. Alexander Whyte of Free St. George's gave a particular tribute to the influence of this book upon him: ". . . Nothing I have read lately is half so good as *With Christ*. Your book goes to the joints and the marrow of things. You are a much honored man: how much, only the day will declare. The other books I have been reading are all able and good in their way, but they are spent on the surface of things. Happy man! You have been chosen and ordained of God to go to the heart of things. I have been sorely rebuked, but also much directed and encouraged by this book."

* * * * *

Working for God

This sequel to *Waiting on God* was first published in 1901, arranged in thirty-one brief chapters for a month's reading. The purpose is "to remind all Christian workers of the greatness and the glory of the work in which God gives us a share. As we see that it is God's own work that we have to work out, that He works it through us, that in our doing it His glory rests on us and we glorify Him, we shall count it our joy to give ourselves to live only and wholly for it."

The author indicated that, beside Christian workers,

three more categories of believers can benefit from its contents: First, those who complain that they are apparently laboring in vain might find the cause of so much failure. "God's work must be done in God's way and in God's power of the Spirit." Second, it is also for another group who practically take no part in the service of their Lord. Murray's position is that "it is God's will that every believer, without exception, whatever his position in life, should give himself wholly to live and work for God." Third, it is also "for those who train others in Christian life and work, that they may find thoughts that will be of use to them in teaching the imperative duty, the urgent need, the divine blessedness of a life given to God's service . . . ."

BIBLIOGRAPHY AND
SOURCE ACKNOWLEDGMENTS

The documentation for the majority of the facts in Andrew Murray's life lies in the two out-of-print biographies listed below. Because the material in the two volumes greatly overlaps, it has not been possible or advisable to interrupt the flow of the narrative of this volume to annotate the sources of the events of Murray's life. The author wishes to express appreciation to these excellent sources, whose publishers have granted permission for use of material from them.

The Life of Andrew Murray of South Africa, by J. Du Plessis. Marshall Brothers Limited, London-Edinburgh-New York, 1919.

Andrew Murray and His Message — One of God's Choice Saints, by Rev. W. M. Douglas. Oliphants Ltd., London-Edinburgh, 1926. Christian Literature Crusade edition, 1957.

Another basic source, particularly for chapters eight and nine, dealing with the early married life of Andrew Murray, is a book not generally known in North America, secured for the author by friends in South Africa. Appreciation is expressed for the use of material from this book, listed below.

Young Mrs. Murray Goes to Bloemfontein (1856-1860), letters edited by Joyce Murray. A. A. Balkema, Cape Town, South Africa, 1954.

Two other sources which I have found useful are:

Unto Children's Children (published for private circulation within the Murray family in 1909). T. H. Hopkins and Son, Ltd., London.

The Joy of Service by Helen Murray (Andrew Murray's sister). Marshall, Morgan and Scott, Ltd., London and Edinburgh, 1935.

I also used information supplied by Mrs. Raymond G. Slater (Charlotte Louise Murray), Andrew Murray's grand niece.

Certain other biographical material has been used, with permission, from:

The South African Dictionary of National Biography, Vol. I, Cape Town, South Africa.

The Encyclopedia of Southern Africa. National Boekhandel, Cape Town, South Africa.

Records of Murray family reunions, obtained from the South African Library at Cape Town.

Court records of the Judicial Committee during the civil suits involving the Dutch Reformed Church and Andrew Murray, published in 1867, located at the South African Library of Cape Town.

Various biographical materials in the Dutch language, located at the University of South Africa at Cape Town.

The author has freely drawn from the text of many of Andrew Murray's books for his teachings, for the imagined answers to questions posed to him in the narrative, and for background material. Prefaces and introductions to most of his books currently in print have been used extensively for the synopses of his books listed in the Appendix. It would be burdensome and distracting to the reader to have the above footnoted or cross-referenced, in fact impossible, because some of the contents of the books overlap in their themes, even in direct quotations.